*What They Don't Teach You at
Theological College*

Malcolm Grundy is the Archdeacon of Craven in the Diocese of
Bradford. He is the author of *Understanding Congregations* and
has led many workshops and seminars on the issues that arise in
this new book.

What They Don't Teach You at Theological College

A practical guide to life in the ministry

Malcolm Grundy

Cartoons by Ron

CANTERBURY
PRESS
Norwich

This book is dedicated to the
clergy and laypeople of the
Diocese of Bradford from whom
I have learned so much

Text © Malcolm Grundy 2003
Cartoons © Ron 2003

First published in 2003 by the Canterbury Press Norwich
(a publishing imprint of Hymns Ancient & Modern Limited,
a registered charity)
St Mary's Works, St Mary's Plain,
Norwich, Norfolk, NR3 3BH
Second impression 2006
www.scm-canterburypress.co.uk

British Library Cataloguing in Publication data

A catalogue record for this book is available
from the British Library

ISBN 1-85311-500-2

Typeset by Rowland Phototypesetting Ltd,
Bury St Edmunds, Suffolk
Printed and bound in Great Britain by

Contents

Part IV: What do you think of it so far?

Preface

Why a book like this?

The clergy of the Church of England have been a part of the fabric of society from the time that Christianity came to our shores. Many clergy have been saints working unrecognized in parish ministry throughout their lives. Others have combined their faith with tremendous reforming energy, bringing schools, hospitals and improved community facilities. Alongside this work goes the caricature of English clergy as objects of fun or ridicule. In an age when church attendance has diminished, many people are now more than a little unsure when they meet 'a vicar'. An introduction to the wider role of Church of England priests is now needed. Furthermore, many clergy themselves are unsure of the inner workings of the Church, which is unlike any other employer. The processes of finding a job, moving on, reviewing one's ministry, or planning for retirement are far from transparent and often seem arcane. This book, which focuses on these and other issues, such as introducing change, would not have happened without the enthusiasm of Christine Smith, Editor for the Canterbury Press, Norwich. From early conversations about the mysterious nature of the workings of the Church, this idea developed and I am most grateful for her encouragement. As an active layperson she has been invaluable in reminding me of the need to explain, in straightforward terms and accessible language, just how this Church functions. Our planning for this book began with the assumption that the ways of the Church of England need a simple guide for laypeople, church officers and clergy. I have attempted to cover key areas as I understand them, without drowning the descriptions in detail. I am grateful to Robin Baird-Smith for permission to use small amounts of material first published by Mowbrays in my *Understanding Congregations*.

The aim of this book is to explore the many ways in which the 'clerical' life is experienced. It may help those who are considering ordination to see if their 'inner promptings' are real and whether they are ready to allow a church selection conference to test that calling. I hope that this book will enable men and women at any stage in their ordained or recognized ministries to reflect on where they are and to discern the appropriate next steps for themselves. But this is not only a book to be read by ordinands and clergy; there are many misunderstandings about life and work in the Church and it is important that lay people understand something about the ways and life of their clergy. This book is for them also.

Feeling a call to public ministry can be an awkward thing to explain to family and friends. It can be confusing and disorienting for the partner of a woman or man with this calling. This book may help those who are friends, family and partners of ordinands and clergy to understand the sometimes confusing and often quaint ways of a church which has claimed so great a part of the person they love and support. Perhaps after reading these pages the mist will have cleared a little.

Many of the descriptions of training for ministry and clerical life come from seminars and discussions with ordinands, clergy and laypeople who have shared their experiences and concerns with me. I will be for ever in the debt of training officers, primarily in Britain and Sweden but also in other parts of Europe and the United States, for the opportunity to listen, share ideas and analyse situations. I hope that these friends will recognize many of our discussions in this book – and forgive any misrepresentations on my part. Many, if not most, of the personal situations in this book apply much more widely than in England and I hope that they will stimulate discussion in other places. I am driven on in my work less by its frustrations and more by the sense that a new Church is being created to sustain new generations. There is an excitement in being part of this work of reconstruction with such stimulating colleagues. The Body of Christ has many parts and I hope that our work may encourage some of them to be a little more 'joined up'.

Malcolm Grundy
Epiphany 2003

Part I

From calling to retirement

Who would be a priest?

Mandy looked forward to ordination with
eager anticipation

All are called

One of the oldest jokes in the Church about the selection of our
clergy is that we only have the laity to choose from! Behind this
there is a much more serious point: that there is only one community
of faithful people who are the Church. What we are asked and
called to carry out are different tasks and responsibilities within
that community.

The place of clergy in the wider world and in the Christian

community has changed, as have political and social attitudes towards them. Wherever a time capsule might land, it would reveal a different and intriguing picture of the place of clergy. In the early Church it is likely that members of the local Christian community elected or appointed one of their number to preside at the eucharist and be a person 'set apart' for particular liturgical and teaching functions. This role was understood as being in succession to the work and actions of Jesus, at first carried on by the apostles and then continued with apostolic authorization and ordination through the laying on of hands. The Catechumenate gave enquirers and new members a grounding in the faith and acted as a filter in times of persecution. Orders of priests and bishops, though not part of New Testament Church, developed a significant place as teachers and guardians of the faith. At the beginning of the fourth century, when the Emperor Constantine gave official recognition to Christianity, the Church had grown to cover much of Europe and some of the East, and the structures we know today had begun to be formed.

The establishment of religious orders gave a different place for men and women as they worked out how to live in community by taking vows of poverty, chastity and obedience. Some in religious orders were priests, while many others were lay brothers and sisters. Missionary outreach gave a new place for bishops, priests and religious orders in spreading the faith. We know that Patrick, Boniface and Sigfrid, among many others, travelled to distant parts of Europe. Sometimes priests and bishops were involved in political activity. Thomas à Becket is perhaps the best known of those 'troublesome' priests and martyrs.

After the Reformation clergy moved away from the celibate life and communities of religious to become the local person or 'parson'. Often now with families, they lived among their people. Services were in the common tongue and church furnishings were simplified. The rise of other denominations, and the continuation of the Roman Catholic Church, has given rise to a much wider expression of priesthood and the clerical life around the world.

Victorian and Edwardian England provided the model of a resident clergyman whose prime focus was the parish (see also below, p. 10, on George Herbert). Although this was the norm for only 150 years, the parish priest has become the accepted ideal. Interestingly, from the seventeenth century onwards many in this situation were scholars, scientists, botanists and men of letters. Their focus was on scholarship and intellectual exploration, often done from a parochial base.

Through the last century the lives of many clergy have been characterized by heroic example. Chaplains in the First and Second World Wars discovered a closer identification with non-church-going people. The same was true of those who pioneered ministries as Worker Priests or industrial chaplains. This work has been done at a time when the overall number of those offering themselves for the priesthood in the West has been declining.

In respect of the place of clergy for today and tomorrow, do we face a crisis of confidence or of the reinterpretation of traditional roles? The meaning of the word crisis in its Greek usage is a 'judgement' rather than a dramatic, tension-filled moment. When we look to the future, the history of our clergy and their place in society give us as much confidence as concern. We are experiencing a revision of the role and place of clergy in the life of our churches. Their valued and special place is not in doubt, but what has to be reconsidered is the question of how we define, select and deploy our clergy.

In many ways clergy are already redefining themselves by how they are choosing to live and express their ministry. Priestly ministry can be parish- or work-based, paid or self-supporting, local or international: the variety is diverse. Many clergy live in a tension somewhere between being priests in the Church they would like to see, and continuing in roles which seem to allow the vestiges of an old, unenergized, Church to continue. That tension can be as creative as it can be frustrating. A very special kind of leadership and oversight is needed to allow this transition towards a renewed Church to continue.

Our journey together

In what follows we shall explore what is involved in the selection of clergy and the work they carry out. Such a description, with analysis, may help those considering ordination and also their families. It might also enable the lay members of congregations to understand their clergy better. While this book reflects my own context of ministry, the Church of England, I hope that at least some of what I have to say and describe will be relevant to anyone considering a particular call in any denomination. It could be useful for any clergy who want to review where they are in their own ministry. Before we look at how clergy are selected and what their life is like, we need to look at the nature of Christian calling and discipleship for all believers who make up the people of God within churches and congregations.

A faith for everyone

Each of us explores and lives our faith every day in countless different ways. Our time is divided between the workaday world, our families, friends and our chosen leisure pursuits. Church membership is what we choose as part of that balance and involves a commitment which will vary at different times in our lives. Participation in the life of a local church has great opportunities for worship, friendship, study and service. The character of a congregation and its impact on a local community depends on the quality and commitment of its members. Lay people are nurtured, cared for, trained and supported by their minister. Together, clergy and lay people share in a modern-day working out of the idea that they are the Body of Christ on earth. Together, they offer up the cares and concerns of their community and the wider world to God in prayer and worship. In doing this they play a small part in the continuing work of Jesus Christ as faith, life work and prayer come together. This way of life, with its commitment to worship and service, is called the 'priesthood of all believers' (Exodus 19.4–6, 1 Peter 2.9f.). It is fundamental to all Christian ideas of priesthood, ministry and service.

Vocation and ministry

People come to faith and work out how they are to live as Christian people in ways which cannot always be articulated. They feel a sense of calling to Christian service and to a way of life which goes with it. We get our word 'vocation' from the Latin word for calling. Our modern usage of the word is open to a misunderstanding. Too often we think of vocation as a calling to some special kind of work, to be a missionary or a doctor or nurse.

The word 'vocation' is interesting in itself. It needs to be unpacked so that we can see the possibilities which are held within its meaning and use. There is a school of thought which has tried to break away from a limited definition and says that the fullest interpretation of vocation is found in how we live all parts of our life as a Christian person. It suggests that we are all called to be Christian people, and what we do as Christians in response to that call is our ministry. One of the clearest unfoldings of this understanding is in the collect which is used at ordination services in the Church of England:

> Lord of all the world,
> we thank you that through your Son
> you have called us into the fellowship
> of your universal Church.
> Hear our prayer for your faithful people
> that each in their *vocation and ministry*
> may be an instrument of your love.

The calling to a particular ministry

It is right for most people that they should do their best to work out what it means to be called to be a Christian wherever they are. Not many are asked to give up their jobs and go off to do something else. It is a hard thing to become a Christian, change some of your behaviour and stay with the people who know you already. Most people will feel prompted to adapt their lives and do their jobs in different ways. Some will feel that they need to find jobs which come closer to the understanding they have of their faith. Many people will say that their lives develop and that their faith changes over time. Within this they choose to change jobs and do things which 'fit' more closely the person they would like to become. Part of the work of the Church, in its local congregations, is to support people through their working lives and in the changes which come as careers and employment develop. Few people would say that the Church is very good at giving its support to people at work, though there have been valiant attempts to understand 'the world of work' by churches, industrial missioners and others who engage in 'workplace ministries'.

Ministries within the Church

There are some people who feel a particular call to ministry within the Church. They have strong internal feelings, prompted by their prayer life, which suggest that they should offer themselves for work which is recognized and accredited by their Church. Contrary to some popular belief, not all those who work for the Church are called to ministry as 'vicars'. In the Church of today – and tomorrow – some will not feel called to work full-time in the parochial ministry, though most will want to do exactly that.

There is a range of ways in which ministry can be exercised in the Church:

- Accredited lay ministry enables a person to be selected and trained in similar ways to clergy. Those in this work remain lay people and are available for deployment into parish or specialist work.
- Work with the Church Army is an opportunity for those who do not want to be ordained to have a full-time, recognized and accredited ministry, primarily as evangelists.
- The permanent diaconate offers an increasing number of people the possibility of a renewed way of working in the Church. Deacons have particular responsibilities in liturgy and in service in the world. There are significant moves to restore the permanent diaconate as a group offering something distinctive to the Church.
- The priesthood remains the most significant option for those who feel a call to work in the Church. Priesthood can be exercised in a stipendiary or non-stipendiary way. It can be a local ministry or part of the wider group of clergy willing to be deployed in different places at different times in their lives.
- The Religious Life is still considered and chosen by an influential group within the Church. There are Anglican Religious Orders for men and women across the country. Some focus on the contemplative life while others are very much in the world. Nowadays most Religious live in small communities, although some are contemplatives who choose to live a solitary lifestyle.

Each of these is a separate and different way of understanding calling to a particular ministry within the Church. The context in which these ministries can be lived and worked out can also vary widely:

- work within a Church of England parish or group of parishes;
- work within a group or team ministry, which may be ecumenical;
- full or part-time work as a specialist minister;
- chaplaincy work in a hospital, school, university or prison, in industry and commerce, or in the armed forces;
- membership of a Religious Order as a priest, deacon or lay person;
- continuing in a secular occupation and exercising a priestly ministry there;
- being non-stipendiary, unpaid and working in a parish or specialist ministry;
- work as a priest within a local ministry team.

Such a range of opportunities is still exciting for many people and a steady and increasing stream of men and women continue to offer themselves for this way of life – which is both vocation and ministry.

How do we know which lifestyle to choose?

It is all very well being presented with a list of ways in which ministry can be worked out. How is it possible to know which one is right for you? The vocations advisers in dioceses are the best people to consult. They will first of all look at your prayer life with you and try to assess whether your calling to priestly or other ministry is of God. You will then be led to look at where you are in your life. It may be that a family can be uprooted and taken with you to a residential college and on to life in another part of the country. It may be that it cannot. This is also a time for guidance towards realism about what is possible for yourself within your vision. This may seem very worldly, but you will have to consider whether you can afford to make the move at this time. You will need to sit down with your family and consider the possible reduction in income and change in lifestyle which may result.

Resources to help in your approach to priestly ministry

There is a great tradition of books about ministry. In this book there will be a focus on priestly ministry, though other ways of responding to a particular call have already been described and will be revisited from time to time. Some books explore priesthood and ministry from the point of view of history and theology. One such book, which still gives both a real and a romantic picture of the priest in a parish, is George Herbert's *A Priest to the Temple*. Here the picture of the visiting, praying, holy parish priest is set out. Its influence as a model of the 'ideal' parish priest is abiding among many clergy and many more lay people – most of whom may have never heard of or read George Herbert's book.

We have an equally honourable modern tradition of theological writing about ministry within the Church. There are significant books like Hans Küng's *Why Priests?*, which maps the key questions facing the priesthood today, or *Ministry* by Edward Schillebeeckx, which looks at the relationship between priesthood and the worshipping community. Others look at the 'nuts and bolts' of how to work as a vicar in a parish; *The Parish Priest Today* by Charles Forder supported many generations of parish clergy. In recent times Robin Greenwood's *Transforming Priesthood* has been widely read and is an informative and theological book about emerging patterns of ministry. His *Transforming Church: liberating structures for ministry* attempts in a realistic and positive way to explore what it will mean in our churches to have a much greater involvement of the whole people of God in local ministry. From the Church of England's 'official' stable, Gordon Khurt has edited and collated *Ministry Issues: mapping the trends for the Church of England*. *Tentmaking* by James M. M. Francis and Leslie Francis is also an important study of how clergy fulfil their ministries in non-church situations where the workplace is central. Most recently Christopher Cocksworth and Rosalind Brown have produced *Being a Priest Today* for the Canterbury Press. My attempt builds on these valuable contributions and I hope that it will take enquirers and practitioners on into the spiritual and practical questions which face all those committed to supporting Christian Ministry for today and tomorrow.

A rich inheritance

There is one enduring and much loved 'classic' book which continues to sell and be reprinted. Through its reflective and learned simplicity it continues to inspire one generation after another, and better books than this will not replace it. Archbishop Michael Ramsey's *The Christian Priest Today* was first published in 1972. It has been reprinted many times and a revised version is still available. It is important to consider the enduring qualities of priesthood which Ramsey identifies before we get on to the practical chapters about a ministerial life.

The qualities of a priestly life

In his hesitant, scholarly, quiet and humble way, through a series of addresses to those about to be ordained in Durham, York and Canterbury, Michael Ramsey set out how he saw the person and work of a priest in the Church. His thoughts and musings offer a fundamental way of thinking about how the priestly life should be formed and ordered. Ramsey wrote in times of scepticism and he was aware that the role of the priest in society had changed. The priest was no longer automatically respected. Clergy in most parishes were no longer those with 'position', knowledge, skills and experience which others did not have. Then, as now, there was an 'anti-institutional' trend in both society and the Church. He saw that many people, some organizations and parts of the press were almost anti-clerical and that, in a prophetic sentence, many lay people wanted 'the church to be a more lively society, with far more spontaneous initiatives in leadership and service'. He realized that a lively laity often saw the existence of a professional ministry group as a hindrance to the creation of a Church for the future where the ministry of all the baptized would be valued. How often do we still hear in our discussion groups and parish weekend workshops a description of the parish priest as the 'bottle-neck' rather than the enabler?

The place of a priest or minister in society

It is fascinating to see how the place of clergy has changed in much of modern society. Similar reactions can be seen in many other parts of the world. The minister or vicar, particularly in the Victorian era, had a central place in society. He was often a leading figure in any community, along with the squire, the teacher and the doctor, although often poorer than his important neighbours. In cities many clergy were pioneering social reformers. In towns and villages they were involved in the administration of the Poor Law and in teaching.

Clergy have not always been popular figures in society. There is a view, developed by Professor A. G. Dickens and others, that clerical unpopularity took some of its modern form in the fifteenth and early sixteenth centuries. His view is that English men and women had a hunger for more satisfying spiritual fare than the formal, clerically dominated religion of medieval Catholicism. This spiritual hunger manifested itself in a kind of anti-clericalism which had its inevitable consequence in the Reformation.

Yet the priest or vicar has also been seen as an integral part of English life, and still is to a certain extent today, particularly in rural areas. In recent years there has emerged a more revisionist view, associated with the studies and writings of scholar-historians like Eamon Duffy, which holds that there was widespread support for traditional worship through Reformation times and beyond. Alongside it went a respect for church and clergy. Duffy's most readable book, *The Voices of Morebath*, uses valuable parish churchwarden's accounts to trace the respected ministry of Sir Christopher Trychay over 52 years of faithful ministry in one Devon parish from 1520 to 1572. His life was a model of the kind of able priest that Michael Ramsey describes in his contemporary picture of the relationship of a priest to the wider society.

There are many instances of clergy families, fathers and sons, holding livings through generations. Archbishop Geoffrey Fisher's great-grandfather was appointed to the living of Higham on the Hill in Leicestershire in 1772. It was subsequently held by his grandfather and his father, their ministry spanning a total of 120 years.

Whatever the judgement of history, there is a real sense today that clergy are separated from society. In some ways this is appropriate and necessary for their ministry. In other ways this separation is a hindrance. Some clergy and laity collude with it in order to establish and keep a safe distance. The whole Worker Priest movement in France and elsewhere in the 1950s and 60s was a bold attempt at identification with working people. It was a move, eventually suppressed by the Roman Catholic Church, to 'bridge the gap'. Ministers in Secular Employment and many Non-Stipendiary Ministers interpret their calling as living in much the same 'alongside' way today.

The formation of a priest

The far-sighted Michael Ramsey saw that in a new situation, all clergy, wherever they placed themselves, would have to display particular qualities. There needed to be a reversal of the hierarchical nature of ordained ministry and a re-focusing on the tasks and person of the priest in a renewed Church. This necessary change would mean an emphasis on what Ramsey describes as the *representative* nature of priesthood. He saw the significance of the priesthood as a gathering up of the roles which belong to the whole people of God. Building on an essay by Alec Graham, later Bishop of Newcastle, he says that the priesthood of the future will have a significance as it develops characteristics that he describes as *displaying, enabling and involving*. By ordination a Christian becomes a particular sign of the ministry of Jesus in the Church. The priest is to be a 'beacon' of the Church's pastoral, prophetic and priestly concern. It is these things which a priest *displays* through the training which is provided and by lifelong attempts at the continuing process of formation into a Christ-like person. From this challenging presentation follow other attributes. A priest *enables* those Christ-like qualities as he, and now she, works 'to get things done' in the Church and in the community in which it is set. More and more often in modern selection criteria the word 'collaborative' appears. While never clearly defined, it can be an ability to draw others into a participative exercise; doing things *with* people rather than *for* them. I explore this much more fully in chapter 13.

This 'collaborative' quality, displayed in the congregation, will mirror the integrated way in which God is known as Father, Son and Spirit. Truth emerges by work done in community. Each priest displays the Christ-like attributes in their own person but works to ensure that these qualities permeate the whole congregation. In doing this the third of Ramsey's characteristics emerges, that of *involvement*. The 'one-person band', the hierarchical model, even the 'command and control' way of running things, are no longer to be the qualities or styles of leadership expected of a priest, if they ever were. There is a new way. It is approached first by personal, internal discipline, followed by the development of a new kind of professionalism which will be likely to gain a respected place in the Church and, equally importantly, in the communities we are all called to serve.

The disciplines of a priest

Underpinning these qualities, which work themselves out in action, are the lifelong disciplines which bind the priest. Michael Ramsey is in his element when he talks of these things. First and foremost the priest is a teacher and a preacher, and as such is a person steeped in whatever it is we all come to call *theology*. This is summed up by Ramsey for the reluctant priest and for the hungry layperson in a wonderful sentence: 'Their study need not be vast in its extent but it will be deep in its integrity, not in order that they may be erudite but in order that they may be simple.'

He then moves our priestly thinking on to suggest that there is a discipline of the *ministry of reconciliation*. In a world of many disciplines, even in the caring professions where the priest will find many colleagues, there is another dimension to add to all the therapy and community development on offer. Through the unfashionable dimension of the concept of sin the priest reveals the work of a forgiving Church. This is brought about by the example of a forgiving Jesus Christ. The ministry of reconciliation has gone beyond the intimacy of the unfashionable and little-used confessional to become one of the few signs that a past can be overcome. Resurrection and liberation come ultimately from the ability to forgive and encourage. Through the bringing together of often seemingly irreconcilable groups in a community the seeds of new life can be sown – the reconciliation of those who would otherwise be kept apart by their lack of ability to forgive, their imprisonment in past memories, guilt, blame and the desire to exact vengeance, is begun. A priest is forever called to seek these possibilities.

For much of the Church's ministry public prayer is expressed through the priest. From both personal desire and public expectation the priest will be a *person of prayer*. In a wonderful phrase Ramsey says that priests will 'be with God with the people on our heart'. The priestly life is one of continuous intercession for the needs of the people among whom they minister. Like Jesus the great High Priest described in the Epistle to the Hebrews, the priest lives to make intercession. Interestingly, Ramsey points out that the Greek verb 'to intercede' does not mean 'to make a pleading for' but 'to encounter, to be with someone on behalf of, or in relation to, others'. Just as Jesus bore the sins of us all upon his heart on Calvary, so the priest who in ordination promises to be 'diligent in prayer' is, in Ramsey's phrase, promising 'to be daily with God with the people on your heart'.

Quite unsurprisingly, Ramsey concludes his unfolding of the possibilities of priestly ministry with a reflection which is the pinnacle of his own spirituality. In all the disciplines of the priestly life this formation leads towards being *the person of the Eucharist.* In the act of presidency at the Lord's table in the Eucharist the priest becomes more than a representative person from the congregation. The celebrant undertakes symbolic acts – taking, thanking, breaking, giving – which are the universal acts of the Eucharist. In saying these words of institution given by Jesus at the Last Supper and by performing the actions, the priest represents the act not of one single congregation but of the whole Holy Catholic Church through the centuries. Christ's Body is offered again in this sacramental way by the priest. In that offering, which is the redemptive act, the forgiving, reconciling, praying, interceding High Priest Jesus Christ becomes incarnate and transforms a world in need. The priestly privilege of presiding over this liturgical act, with historic continuity and present-day reality, is the greatest of all relationships for those who are called to minister in it.

Too great a task?

Do these descriptions of ministry in the Church put off any reader who is considering ordination? In one way they should, but this should not deter the aspirant. No minister, even one who has celebrated 50 years or more, would claim to have achieved all, or even a measure, of the vision.

Do you aspire to it? Are you enlivened by the thought of it? Are you humbled by the challenge and the impossibility of it? If you can answer 'yes' to that cascade of questions, then you might be ready to consider the life of a deacon, priest, religious or lay minister in the Church. Michael Ramsey's tasks of displaying, enabling and involving take a lifetime; they are a lifelong attempt to work at theology, at intercession for and within the needs of the world. They can come in a lifelong, Christlike ministry of reconciliation for priests who accept the privilege of repeated presidency at the Eucharist. In a last and telling phrase from Ramsey, 'we commend ourselves if our consciousness is not of our own status but of Christ whose commission we hold and of the people we serve in his name'.

2

The selection process

They already had his name down for Mirfield

Here am I, send me

There comes a time when your inner feelings and the casual suggestions of others about the priesthood have to be tried out. You know that your sense of calling to ministry in the Church has to be shared with someone. I always liken this to pressing on a door to see if it will open. Many clergy will remember this moment vividly. If there is a close friend, a partner, a parent or a priest to share the idea with, then the testing of a calling to this ministry can begin. It is from family and friends that the most difficult response may come. A partner can be settled in a home and a job of their own and this will spell disruption. Parents can have other expectations for you. They may have seen your education as leading to a well-paid job or profession. The relatively low pay, long hours and lowly prospects of ministry will not necessarily seem so attractive to outsiders, family and friends.

Many other people will say that they received a different response. The sharing of a feeling that ordination might be a future path is met with a sense of satisfaction and relief. There may well have been hopes that you would feel a call to ministry. Sometimes members of a local church are delighted that one of their number is offering themselves for ministerial training. They have yet to realize that if you move away and take your family, a considerable hole will be left in the life of their local congregation!

There is another response to ordination which you will have to weigh more sensitively. It may be that you have felt pressured towards this decision. If you are involved in the life of your local church, or even more widely, you could have had the idea of ordination suggested to you. There is the mistaken assumption that commitment to a life of faith and activity within a local church automatically suggests the path to ordination.

What you will have to explore is whether your own particular calling to ministry should lead to this work in the Church. There is a danger that what is attracting you is the example of clergy you know, or those you see or read about. The only way to be anything or anybody is to 'be yourself'. I have been a senior selector of clergy for many years now. The main piece of guidance which I give to myself and the other selectors is to look for an answer to only one question, 'Is God calling *this person* to be a priest?'

The selection process

At some stage early in the discernment process any potential ordinand has to share their feelings and their questioning with their vicar. This is the normal pattern of what is technically called 'preselection'. Most clergy will be receptive to such a conversation and ready to advise on what to do next. In just a few cases your vicar may not agree with your idea. You will have to take what they say seriously; but if you disagree, then you will need to share your thoughts with someone else. This may be a priest you know in another parish or part of your life. You can also ask to see a vocations adviser or the Diocesan Director of Ordinands (DDO). Some women who feel called to ordination will not be able to share their ideas with their parish clergy if they are opposed to the ordination of women to the priesthood, though most will be courteous and refer you to someone who can advise.

Almost all dioceses will have one or more people designated as vocations advisers. They will give you some initial advice and talk your ideas through with you. Many organize vocations days or even weekends, where those who are giving thought to initial ideas about ministerial training can come together, share ideas and misgivings, and receive information and advice. Sometimes these diocesan events simulate the selection conference method itself. This may sound terrifying but I want to encourage you to see it as a help. You will discover that the whole experience, including the searching questions of others, can help you to explore whether your initial thoughts were the development of romantic ideas, caused by the over-prompting of others, or if there is something real which demands further exploration.

Everyone who wants to offer themselves for a recognized ministry in the Church of England has to have that sense of calling to particular work recognized by other members of the Church. Local commendation would normally come from your vicar and your Parochial Church Council. The type of selection route you take will depend on the type of ministry you want to have.

Residential selection conferences

After local selection you undertake a process which allows the Church as a whole to recognize your call. In the Church of England this work is organized by the staff of the Ministry Division of the Archbishops' Council. The selection processes may differ slightly according to the kind of ministry for which you are offering, because all selection is in a real sense 'advisory'. It is the bishop of your diocese, the person who admits everyone to ministry through his office as bishop, who will make the ultimate decision about your selection and training. Most bishops accept the advice of local selection panels and the selection conferences of the Ministry Division, but they are free to make their own decisions after weighing the advice they have been given, which is always backed up by written evidence.

Residential selection conferences have a standard pattern. Your path to one of these will be a recommendation from your Diocesan Director of Ordinands. One of the Ministry Division secretaries will liaise about your own timetable and availability, having sent you a range of papers to read and some (more!) forms to fill in. There is a diagram of the selection process at the end of this chapter. It may well be that in the quite near future more selection will be done by dioceses and less through nationally organized conferences.

What is a conference like?

Conferences are all held at diocesan retreat or conference centres. One reason for this is to ensure absolute confidentiality. If another group was also resident, or you were in a hotel, there would be too much scope for distractions. Dress is informal, though it is best not to be over-casual. Wear the clothes which will make you feel at ease but also help to present you in the best way, as who you really are!

Many candidates are anxious about when they are being interviewed or observed, but it is stressed that the worship, meals and free time are not part of the selection process. Each conference has two people, one ordained and one lay, who act as joint chairs. One of them will introduce the programme in the first session. A selection secretary is responsible for running the event and will have all the relevant papers. The selectors will be responsible for conducting the worship, so you are completely free to use the chapel, and the liturgies, for your own prayers.

In the present pattern you will be in a group with half the members of conferences for most of the time. There are four different elements in the two days you spend together. The first is a series of interviews. Each of you will have the opportunity to spend up to 50 minutes with the senior selector and the educational and pastoral selectors. In a structured discussion, they will explore different areas of your life and calling. Each will have read the preparatory papers which you and your DDO have submitted.

Between interviews you will be asked to produce a short written piece on a subject that will be given to you. This is to see how well you can express yourself in writing and to explore your ideas and reasoning on a particular subject. Alongside this is an exercise for all of you to engage in together. It is a kind of 'role play' where different aspects of a situation have to be discussed as a group, and each member is given the chance to chair a discussion. Finally, you will have to undertake a kind of IQ test called a 'cognitive exercise', intended to help the selectors decide what pattern of training might suit you best.

Once candidates have left the conference the selectors remain overnight to make their recommendations. It is always stressed that the conference is not an occasion when candidates pass or fail an examination. Most people find selection conferences helpful – let me assure you of this if you are at the outset of the process. Those who come seem to bond together very quickly and most are seen exchanging email or postal addresses as they leave. The selectors are not meeting to discuss whether you have passed or failed. They are trying to discern if God is calling you to be a priest. On each of the set occasions when they met you they made notes: it is vital that every opinion they express is backed up with written evidence and they will come to a decision about each candidate they meet. A candidate can be recommended unconditionally; recommended with mandatory conditions for further development; not recommended, with reasons why they are being given this decision at this time; or simply not recommended. Under normal circumstances, no-one can return to a selection conference within a period of two years.

Alongside the recommendation comes a written report which is sent to your diocesan bishop and your director of ordinands. These reports are confidential but your bishop and DDO will share this information with you. With the recommendation comes a suggested course for training. A conditional recommendation is accompanied by the 'conditions'. Your DDO will have to supervise you through whatever it is you need to do before training can begin.

A 'not recommended' will also come with its reasons. This subject is the most delicate to be shared and requires much pastoral sensitivity on the part of all concerned for the decision to be accepted after so many high hopes. There are some who never accept the decision. Others can see the wisdom of what has been said, usually from the perspective of a few months or years. There will be some who, with some further training, experience or development, will decide to come to another selection conference. It is essential that the issues raised at the first conference have been addressed by the time a person comes to a subsequent conference.

Dishing the dirt

What are selectors looking for in a candidate? Certainly not the perfect Christian! They do want to see the real you, so there is no point in pretending things about yourself or not revealing your own thoughts about your faith. They are looking for someone who can express why they feel called to be a *priest*. Some people who get to conferences have not been active Christians for very long and need a wider vision of the role of a priest. There are others who have only the experience of their own local congregation and whose concept of priesthood is limited or distorted. There are many who come without working out the difference between an active lay person, even a full-time, paid lay person in the church, and a priest.

The selectors will be trying to discover a person who prays and reads their Bible. It will help if you can show that you have a regular pattern of prayer and that you use some of the prayer forms and Offices of the Church of England. You will not need to demonstrate that you can quote texts from the Bible but it is important that you study the Bible regularly and that you use some form of 'notes' to help you. The use of a 'quiet time' each day shows that you are developing a varied prayer life. You should have a spiritual director or someone you use regularly to advise and guide you in your spiritual development.

All the modern guidance for selectors asks them to observe how well you work with others. They need to see that you have the potential to develop the important collaborative skills. They are not looking for individualists who will plough their own furrow come what may. The Church of today and tomorrow needs clergy who will be able to co-ordinate multi-parish pieces of work. Consequently it is essential that they can share out work, delegate, and enthuse others to carry out tasks which the vicar might well have done in former times.

You can still be ordained if you are not in favour of the ordination of women to the priesthood. There are separate selection conferences for those who hold these views. There are also separate ordination services and training parishes. Most dioceses will expect such ordinands to join in training and other events with curates and diocesan clergy who do support the ordination of women.

Discernment or selection?

A selection conference is not an examination, though it may feel like this as you approach it. For the Christian, life is a continuous process of waiting on God for guidance and direction. Often this support and movement comes through relationships with other people. For each and every one of us, life is a journey in which our spirituality and self-understanding change and develop. We are in a continuing process of formation and re-formation.

Your selection conference is a part of that continuing process. At this stage in your Christian journey, often through a series of events in your personal life, you have come to a point where this exploration of ministry is right. What happens in the chain of events from talking to your family, friends and vicar right up to the selection conference and letter, or meeting with your bishop, is a process of exploration. With others, you have been accompanied through a process where you yourself, alongside those appointed and trained for the work, have taken a look at where you are in life, where you are with God, and what you might be ready to do for the future.

Mistakes can be made

Do selectors always get it right? Of course not. There are many deeply hurt people in our Church who do not accept the recommendation of the conference or the decision of their bishop. We are all fallible and there is no doubt that some of those who have not been recommended were unfairly judged at that time. Selectors, and even bishops, cannot completely know the mind of God. They can only make their best attempt, within their competence and with due humility, to come to the best decision they can. If there is doubt then there is always the possibility that a candidate may return to another conference.

The other side of such a dilemma is that some people will be accepted for training and subsequently ordained who should not have been. It is not always kind to let candidates through if the selectors are not sure. There are clergy who are unhappy in their ministry because they were led by others to offer themselves, or persuaded themselves wrongly, for whatever reasons, that they wanted to be ordained. They, their families and their parishioners come to suffer unnecessarily as a result.

A proven process

It is a great privilege to have such a process available to you. As a selector I have a dream that all Christians might have such a 'discernment package' available to them. Every believer needs a series of accompanied ways in which their particular calling and ministry can be explored at different times in their lives. For ordinands, this is what happens. Some will have to come to terms with vocational guidance which decides that they are not called to the particular ministry for which they have offered themselves. Others will have their call recognized and begin the path through training towards their next sphere of ministry.

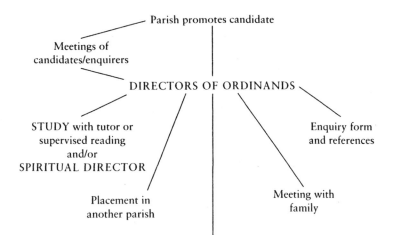

Parish promotes candidate

Meetings of
candidates/enquirers

DIRECTORS OF ORDINANDS

STUDY with tutor or
supervised reading
and/or
SPIRITUAL DIRECTOR

Enquiry form
and references

Placement in
another parish

Meeting with
family

If ordination seems to be the right course

Interview with Bishop before
being sponsored

Sponsoring papers
(prepared by DDO)

Briefing meeting
about conference

SELECTION CONFERENCE

REPORTS AND RECOMMENDATION

Conditionally recommended
DDOs work out
how to fulfil condition
in collaboration
with Board of Ministry

Not recommended
Meeting with DDO
to discuss way forward

Recommended

COLLEGE or COURSE
support offered by DDOs including working out
budget for residential training

**Figure 2.1 The process leading to selection and training for
the ordained ministry in the Church of England**

3

Patterns of training:
colleges and courses

... and as the makers point out, one size fits all

For some people college days, like school-days, can seem to be the best days of your life. Very many clergy refer back to their training as a time of importance and significance. It is not unusual to hear the words of college principals or deans quoted half a lifetime later as still having formative significance for some clergy.

Once a person is recommended by a selection conference, and often before, a programme of training is planned. The Diocesan Director of Ordinands will advise which type of training will best suit a candidate. The selectors will have looked at the same question. On some occasions, but not very often, a student will be at a college before the selection conference takes place. Most people will begin their training at an appropriate time after they have been recommended and their bishop has made his own decision about them. This decision may also affect the choice of college and pattern of training. Recommendation is *the* key to the funding of ordination training.

Colleges and courses

There are two types of training available for most ordinands in the Church of England: residential theological colleges and courses which allow students to continue in their secular occupations. The choice of a college or course is determined by agreement based on an ordinand's academic needs or possibilities and their personal and family circumstances.

Residential theological colleges

Residential colleges are in different parts of the country and are all associated with a university or institute of higher education. Courses are said to be 'tailor-made' for students, but when I checked this out with some who had completed such courses the question provoked cynical laughter! Clearly, theological college cannot arrange to teach you all you need to know. On the other hand, I am very well aware of the sensitive arrangements made for those who go into residential study.

Training lasts from one to three years according to a person's age and previous academic background. Many lectures are held in the residential college; others will be in the external college to which the theological college is affiliated. Some training is in an ecumenical setting, while other parts are very much contained within the 'ethos' of a particular party or tradition within the Church.

All colleges make provision for families to come and live close by. In many places housing is available to rent or buy. The regime within a college provides a regular pattern of study, meditation and worship. This can be fine for single students but is sometimes a severe handicap or discipline for married people with families. Most colleges have worship on Sunday and weekday occasions when families are welcome.

The curriculum and ethos of a college will be set by the college staff in association with trustees, governing bodies and the Ministry Division. There is often tension about how the life of a residential college should be ordered. Each college is an independent charitable foundation but has to gain validation for its courses from the Ministry Division as well as from its associated validating college or university.

Many people will say that the community life of a residential theological college, with its 'monastic' routine of Daily Offices and regular celebrations of the Eucharist, sets a pattern which they will want to follow for the rest of their lives. Critics say that this 'monastic' routine is inappropriate as a training for the spirituality required in a busy parochial ministry. Equally, colleges where the worship is free and informal, even 'touched by renewal', are open to the criticism that students are not sufficiently prepared for the culture shock of more traditional styles of worship in the parish churches where they will serve. The study and practice of liturgy is an essential ingredient of all college and course programmes.

Non-residential courses

Life on a course is a quite different experience. This method of training, which can last for three years, is undertaken while students continue with their secular occupation and remain living at home. Courses are organized regionally and can draw students from a wide area. In a termly pattern meetings will be on one weekday evening. In addition there are weekend residential sessions and summer schools.

For these courses students will come from a wide range of backgrounds and styles of churchmanship. Some courses also have an ecumenical ingredient. Many people have come to see this pattern of training as advantageous because it does not remove a person from their local setting. Indeed, it is hoped that much work experience is brought to bear on the theological content of the training. Critics say that such training does not allow for sufficient academic rigour and does not give the pattern of spiritual discipline which can come in a residential setting.

In the Church of England about half of those in training engage in each pattern. There is a great debate raging about appropriate training. It is likely that the rigid 'one or the other' division will break down and a more mixed series of strands for training will emerge.

Pastoral training

There are many opportunities for ordinands in any method of training to experience and reflect on the types of situation they may encounter in their future ministries. Each course offers the opportunity to spend some time in local situations. Inner-city and multi-faith communities provide experience of major contemporary urban problems. Students are likely to find themselves in hospitals, prisons, work projects for the unemployed, drug rehabilitation centres, on farms and in factories. On Sundays, for a part of their courses, ordinands will assist in worship and preaching. Longer-term parish placements offer experience of ecclesiastical situations and traditions which are unfamiliar to a student's background. In all this the Pastoral Tutors in colleges and courses will use their reflective skills to help students to deepen their understanding of the situations to which they have received some exposure.

Funding for training

In common with all engagement with higher education, theological education is harder and harder to fund. Principal grants come from the Ministry Division. Smaller amounts, for the support of families and the purchase of some books, come from the diocese. There can be little doubt that the Church will have to continue to review the cost of its theological education as its funds become limited and its costs continue to rise.

Students themselves need to budget their costs very carefully. For some, this is a 'starry eyed' time when provision for a long-term future is not at the top of their priorities. I would suggest that every student gets the best financial advice possible. No family should come out of the property market unless they absolutely have to. Many more people are coming into ministry at a later age and will not be able to qualify for a full pension from the Church of England Pensions Board. Even with the pension from their previous employment, they may find it difficult to fund themselves into an adequate retirement. The retention of a house, or the replacement of a present one with something of a more modest size, could be the best security investment for the future.

The purpose of training

What I have never heard expressed by a college or course, what they really don't tell you, is what it is all for. There are many statements of aims, indeed one of the requirements of a college or course is that it should have a statement of aims. These are needed when a course is accredited and when a college is visited by House of Bishops' Inspectors.

Theological training will certainly give students facts. It will give the more able a certain apparatus for approaching academic subjects and equip a student to research a subject and write or make a presentation on it. The training will also provide an immersion into certain social and industrial situations. It will broaden a student's experience of worship and, hopefully, equip them to lead public worship in an orderly and imaginative way.

The purpose of time spent in theological training, in addition to these describable and measurable things, is to develop a framework for thinking and personal development which will last throughout ministerial life. Students learn, in a guided way, how to approach a subject and explore its origins and implications. This technical apparatus is essential for practitioners as they are plunged into a multiplicity of local situations. The life of an ordained person in a parish is full of new situations which crowd in on one another. A minister moves from the joy of a birth to the bedside of a seriously ill person to a youth club or a PCC meeting, sometimes in the space of one day. They will have another ten different situations to enter on the way. To be able to cope with all this and respond in a way which offers something to the person encountered, ministers need to *absorb* within themselves ways of coping, thinking, being objective and bringing the experience into their spiritual consciousness. These tools and this way of thinking and being begin to be learned and absorbed at theological college.

Sponsoring dioceses

Each ordinand or potential ordinand has to be recommended to a selection conference by a diocese. They will remain in relationship with this diocese throughout their training, even if they are not going to work there when their course has ended.

Diocesan Directors of Ordinands are the people who maintain a local relationship with a student throughout his or her training. They also remain in contact with, and support, a student's family throughout the time of training. They may well organize weekends, get-together days and social events for students and their families.

The bishop of the diocese, or one of the suffragan or assistant bishops, will also foster a particular relationship with ordinands. One bishop may have this responsibility in a diocese, or in the larger ones an area bishop may feel a personal responsibility for the ordinands in his own area.

At some stage in the last year of training (my computer spellcheck has also suggested tainting!) a student will know if their home diocese will offer them a title and a training parish. Similarly, a student will inform their sponsoring diocese if they do not want to work in a parish there. In the next chapter we shall look at what is involved in finding a place to work and live, and how to 'read between the lines' in what is said about appointments. There is, of course, a rich anecdotal, but sometimes very real, folklore of horror stories about finding training parishes, the appropriateness of curates' housing, training incumbents and much more. Most of this comes from experience; only some of it is told in theological colleges and courses.

4

Life as a curate

The new curate was sent for a dozen Hail Marys

Finding your training parish

A time comes when the life of a student, and even the luxury and hopes of an ordinand, must eventually come to an end. If there have been continuing uncertainties about ordination, these now have to be faced. As the last year at college or in a course begins, then the discussions about finding training parishes and curacies also begins. Immediately the quaintness of the Church of England begins to become apparent. You are not really looking for 'a job' and you will not be earning a salary or wage. Clergy have 'livings' and they receive a 'stipend'. All of this dates from at least the sixteenth century, when clergy were no longer kept by the lord of the manor or a religious house nor did they have their own land to farm. Local tithes were severely curtailed and there had to be some way of keeping the secular clergy and their new families.

A living is the freehold right to a benefice or parish and the sum of money which is settled in trust on it. Nowadays, of course, livings are standardized and there are stipend bands within which clergy are paid. But they are not paid a wage. A stipend is thought of more as an allowance. This sum will allow a clergyperson to carry out their duties without undue need. With a living also come the rights which go with occupation of the parsonage house or vicarage in a parish. All clergy must reside within their parishes unless given permission by their Bishop to do otherwise.

Junior clergy have to serve a 'title' as an assistant to a stipendiary priest before they can have a parish of their own. Curates come to assistant posts in this way. They also receive a stipend. This is just lower than that of the parish clergy and steps up to nearly or exactly that sum over four years. A house free of rent and rates is also provided, usually by the diocese rather than the parish. Curates' houses are normally three-bedroomed. Vicarages have to have four bedrooms and a study by the front door downstairs. There is a national 'Green Book' guide which sets out the standards expected.

Selecting a parish

Some dioceses are very protective of their ordinands and want to keep them. DDOs will make contact early in a student's final year and begin to discuss a possible parish. In a similar way college principals or a member of staff will begin to talk with students about where they will go to work. Those unplaced by the end of the calendar year before their ordination have their names placed on a national deployment list by the Ministry Division.

A parish will very likely produce a profile so that any prospective student can gain an early impression before they decide to make an initial visit. The origin of such a profile is that each diocese decides which of its clergy could be, or already are, training incumbents. These are clergy who it is thought will be able to accept and work with a junior colleague and help to shape their initial years in ministry. Many dioceses provide training courses for such clergy.

Looking at any parish, either for an incumbency or for a curacy, is a sophisticated business. As a rule of thumb, it is unwise for clergy or ordinands to make a visit if they are very unsure about whether they want to work there. It is hard to say no, once friendly contacts have been made. It is even harder if two or more visits have been made.

Deciding on where to work is a strange mixture of the rational and formal and the intuitive. The parish has to be right and what a prospective curate may be looking for. The house has to be adequate for a family. Many people coming into curacies have growing families and actually need houses as big or bigger than the vicarage. Other factors are more about 'chemistry'. There is a 'feel' to any place, positive or negative, as well as the impressions of the potential new vicar and family. If there seem to be tensions right from the start, it is better to pull out after a first visit. Equally, a training incumbent may say no to any curate for similar reasons.

Eventually a 'right' parish is found. It is normal for the diocesan bishop or area bishop to make the formal offer of a curacy, and the student also makes his or her reply to the bishop, even if letters have been exchanged with the incumbent and DDO.

Preparations for ordination

Ordination is a time of great excitement and anticipation. Everything hoped for over many years is about to come to fruition. It is also a time of great anxiety and transition. Almost as many changes are going to come to the partner, if there is one, as to the ordinand.

The most important change for everyone is that you all become 'public figures', but not public property! Many people will want to meet you. Everyone in the congregation will seem to know all about you. Your house is not your own. People are usually very kind and come round with all sorts of presents. Most will expect to be invited in and shown around. This works well for extroverts and very friendly people. It is an agony to the shy and a nightmare for some partners and children. The phone begins to ring and will not cease until retirement.

Most clergy work from home, though some now have an office

in the church or a parish office in a separate place. It is a great joy to have a study where all the books can be set out. The inevitable computer will be installed and a new lifestyle is about to begin. Parishes pay all a curate's expenses and for some pieces of equipment. The Inland Revenue recognizes that studies are workplaces and take the costs of heating and lighting into account when tax allowances are calculated. All bills should be kept.

The retreat and ordination service

Every bishop holds a retreat for his about-to-be deacons and priests. This may begin after the Thursday ordination service rehearsal at the cathedral and will go right through to the Sunday service. The bishop will invite someone to conduct the ordination retreat and will come himself to give a 'charge'.

The retreat is often a good and reflective experience. Ordinands and deacons can spend some time of quiet preparing themselves for these momentous events. For the family this is the worst time. They may just have moved into a new house and relations and friends will be coming in or to stay, but the star of the show is not there! *They* are in tranquil silence while the family is in chaos.

In contrast, for the single person this is a very different time of transition. From the friendship and community of college or the security of a familiar job a new kind of isolation now comes. While single people are surrounded by the busyness of parish life, they can still feel very much alone. The support of friends far away will be very important. Fending off the over-friendly in the parish will require new skills and the ability to create appropriate boundaries.

Ordination services are normally very special times. In a cathedral or parish church they have a dignity and significance of their own. They unfold well and have a liturgical structure of their own. The sermon comes at the beginning after the 'vocation and ministry' collect already quoted (p. 7). The litany is sung and regarded either as well done or intrusive. Then comes the Making of Deacons, the giving of a New Testament and the placing of the stole across the shoulder. This is followed by the Ordaining of Priests. Their stoles are uncrossed, hung around the shoulders, and a Bible is given. A joyful but restrained sharing of the Peace is followed by the Eucharist.

It is never quite easy to manage the social side of ordinations.

The privileged, families and some parishioners, get tickets for the service. Afterwards there is a lovely time of photographs on the cathedral green or wherever. Most parishes then put on a party back home later in the day. Those who have been ordained priest will celebrate their first Eucharist on the same evening or at some time during the week. Deacons will take their first Services of the Word and will preach. The joy or the agony of pitching the right note at Matins or Evensong will be overcome.

You are a vicar! Well, you know that you aren't really, but everyone else regards you as such. You are wearing your dog collar so you must be a vicar. You will experience the strange renegotiating of relationships which comes with ordination. You will feel that you are just the same person and so will your family, but you and everyone else will also get used to you being the different person, someone set apart yet always accessible, someone who has answered a call and, if your humility remains, someone who will always wonder if they can really do this.

Work in the parish

The new routine begins immediately. A training incumbent will normally work out any priorities and any special areas of responsibility with their curate. It is certainly best that the congregation also knows which areas of work have been designated and to whom. Regular weekly staff meetings should be regarded as fundamental in a training parish.

Some very new experiences will come to a curate. Many will visit their first bereaved people, all will take their first funerals, and the training incumbent should guide these experiences in a sensitive way. A visit to the local crematorium to find out the entrance and the exit and the buttons to be pressed can relieve much anxiety. Baptisms may be performed and after priesting will come the first marriages. Rehearsals and preparation are essential. The joy of such pastoral contacts has to be experienced to be believed. All work in what are called the Occasional Offices is a privilege.

Post-Ordination Training

Universally called 'potty training', the years after ordination are still times of great learning, but now no longer theoretical but done 'on the job'. A new person in the diocese, the Director of Post-Ordination Training, comes on the scene. This person will convene regular meetings of those in the first years of ministry. A course will be devised and visiting speakers will be mixed with discussion and debate. The friendship of new colleagues going through the same experiences can be very supportive.

Deanery and diocese

Further initiation takes place for the newly ordained as they attend chapter meetings of clergy in the deanery, deanery synods and then diocesan synods. These events have a varying element of continuing colleagueship, discussion, debate and frustration. It is generally held that not to attend is worse than attending regularly!

Another destination

Not everyone is called at work as a stipendiary ordained minister. NSM is the usual abbreviation for Non-Stipendiary Ministers. There are those who feel a definite call to the diaconate or priesthood but who are sure that their ministry should be unpaid and more flexible. Some people continue with their everyday jobs; these are called Ministers in Secular Employment or MSEs. They will often be available to do supporting work in parishes during their free time and on Sundays. Many would want to say that their main focus is in the place where they work. The complaint is often made that an MSE is valued by their congregation and vicar more for the time they spend on church matters than for what they do at work.

We are moving very rapidly towards conclusions which make such labels unacceptable. For many years there has been unhappiness with the perception that the stipendiary clergy were a 'higher grade' than those who were unpaid or modern versions of Worker Priests. It is now becoming clear that such distinctions are unhelpful, and even damaging, to the way in which NSMs and MSEs are valued.

Some people have a different kind of calling to ministry recognized. These people are in a local congregation or group of parishes and intend to remain there. Ordained Local Ministers, or OLMs as they are called, intend to do just that. In about half of the dioceses in England there are programmes which bring lay people together in local ministry teams. From these, in some schemes, a person is selected and called to ordination. In other schemes a local person offers themselves just for ordained work in a locality or particular parish. Controversy surrounds such priests. Are they of a different kind because they are not redeployable? Some would say yes, others would say that in the Universal Church, once a priest always a priest and that ministry is related to episcopal authorization and not to place.

Orders and ordination in a changing church

There are three Orders in the Church – bishop, priest and deacon – and these do not relate to method of remuneration or to where that ministry is exercised. It will still take some time for a parochial, congregationally focused Church to recognize and value the equal contribution of all the ordained. The world of the clergy is changing. Overall, there has been an enormous reduction in the number of those responding to a call to ordination and work in the parochial ministry. There are certainly many who have considered a call but have felt that they can serve God in another profession or through other work. Sadly in many ways, there are a significant number of priests who have begun work in the parochial ministry but chosen not to continue. More work needs to be done on the reasons for this.

Interestingly, there are many men and women who do respond to the call to priesthood but who do not want their primary focus to be located in the parochial ministry. They feel a call to chaplaincy within institutions, in the life of a local community or in the workplace. There are also economic reasons why some do not choose to remain in the stipendiary parochial ministry. These diversities of response are causing the Church a significant dilemma at the moment. Officially, and in the places where money is allocated nationally and in dioceses, the emphasis for placing priests is on the parochial ministry. In contrast, and despite the declining numbers, the Church as a national institution is slow to recognize that a significant number of priests feel called to work out their ministry elsewhere. Mission and ministry go together. If many whose ministry is not within the 'official' or 'paid' Church are developing significant new methods of mission and outreach, then there needs to be in the near future a reappraisal of a national strategy for the use and deployment of priests.

I am certain that the local, residential congregation will continue to be the place where worship is offered Sunday by Sunday and on other days. I am equally certain that there is a proven need for church buildings to be an integral part of every community. Place is important in the expression of spirituality and religion. It is more and more likely that these buildings will be wholly maintained by congregations of lay people. The scarce priests, some of them stipendiary, serving clusters of congregations, but many at work in the world, will become valued for their particular gifts and training. The 'Jack of all trades' person-around-to-do-the-odd-jobs-all-week kind of use of the clergy cannot come to an end too quickly. A re-valued priesthood with a distinctive, if specialized, role within the congregation and community might well become a place where more will feel able to respond. I am sure that the call to ordination is much wider than its current interpretation demonstrates.

5

Navigating the appointments system

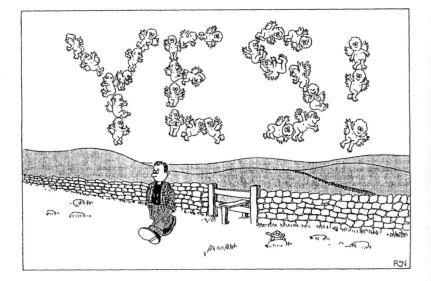

Racked by indecision, Toby sought Divine guidance

A quick glance at the church press will show that there are many different ways of finding a job as a priest. Advertisements in the one edition I scanned for examples show that it is possible to apply for posts as diverse as rector, vicar, team vicar, priest-in-charge, associate minister, senior priest, house for duty priest, chaplain, county ecumenical officer, tutor in church history/liturgy and the history of doctrine(!), stewardship adviser, adult education officer, a missioner or a diocesan director of education. The advertisement might be straight down the line, gimmicky, coded or almost wholly secretive. Just how does it all work and where should clergy go to find a first job, or any job at all? Do we have any kind of regularized system for making appointments? Those involved in the dioceses or as national advisers will say that things have improved tremendously in the past 30 years. In the old days appointments used to be made by 'a word in your ear', or through the network of contacts and acquaintances which bishops and college principals accrued. These valuable 'inside' relationships enabled the 'right' people to be found for vacancies. In reality both advertising and networking operate in an intertwined way in the Church of today.

Appointments in the parochial system

The whole of England is covered by Church of England parishes. Every square inch is regarded as a part of the spiritual care or 'cure' of an Anglican clergyperson. Parishes come in every possible shape and size. They demand an impossible range of talents and skills from clergy to respond to their many-faceted needs. Given a choice, every committed lay person is likely to say that they would like their own vicar in their parish. Most would like to know him or her in a personal way and would certainly want to think that their vicar would 'be available' if they had a particular need or crisis in their life. It is the responsibility of bishops and archdeacons, private patrons and patronage trusts to provide clergy cover for all their territory and to ensure that a named person has the 'cure of souls' in each and every one of these places.

Appointments then and now

There is one big new difference in attitude to appointments today. For many years, perhaps for all the time since the beginning of preferment in the Church, junior and parochial clergy waited for their bishop to suggest a move. Generations would have regarded it as 'bad form' to ask for a move and, even worse, to ask for a particular parish. Indeed, there is still a feeling that the person involved in an appointment should be the last to find out. To ask to be considered for a vacancy is still felt to be almost a black mark against a possible candidate. This system is still writ large over senior appointments of archdeacons, deans and bishops. Recent reports about the senior appointments system and the lifestyle and expenses of bishops have pointed to change, though it is difficult to detect from where that change will be initiated.

Today, more and more clergy would like the opportunity to apply for appointments in open competition. Specialist posts are almost all advertised but this is not yet the case with parish vacancies. Almost every group of parishioners I meet would like to interview several candidates for the post of their new vicar. They are sometimes confronted with a bishop or patron who expresses the thought that they would be deeply affronted if a congregation called into question their pastoral judgement in knowing their clergy and their ability to suggest the 'right' person for any parish. All too frequently, in a modern deployment situation of several parishes being cared for by the same clergyperson, the problem is that no one appointment could possibly fit the demands of differing parishes.

Compass bearings and the appointments system

Yes, there is a system and a national structure for appointing clergy to parishes. It is administered centrally and very many clergy have been grateful for the assistance it gives. There is a public system for filling parish vacancies by advertising publicly for candidates. An increasing number of vacancies are advertised and it is becoming a common occurrence for short-lists of candidates to be offered to parish representatives and even to wider interview panels. The Church of England still has a system, stemming from the sixteenth century, of private patrons who are able to present candidates to bishops for vacant freehold livings which they 'own'. Some patrons are ancient university colleges; others are church party trusts of one kind or another; a few patrons are local groups of trustees. Some parishes have the vicar or rector of their 'mother' or founding church as patron. The great majority of livings are in the gift of the diocesan bishop or a diocesan Board of Patronage. There are also parishes across the country where the patron is the Crown or the Lord Chancellor. Here, particularly, the relationship between Church and State in England is embodied.

The Clergy Appointments Adviser

There is a full-time person with an administrative staff and an office in London whose job in the Church of England is to help clergy find new posts. Clergy who think that the time is approaching for a move can arrange an interview. There is also a regular series of opportunities around the country for clergy to meet the Adviser. Curates looking for a first living or staff appointment can also use this service. Following an initial form filling, the interview can then help the person looking for a move to think through where they are now and what they might do next.

The list

A confidential list of those asking for a move is circulated to diocesan bishops and their staff each month. The papers contain details of the person wanting a move, their family situation, their ministerial history and academic achievements, churchmanship and, most significantly for senior staff members, the areas of the country in which they are prepared to serve. A commendation is given by the clergyperson's present bishop or his representative and extracts are given from references as well as from the person's own description of their ministry. The full confidential sets of references are available on request. Names remain current on this list for one year, and a list of those placed is also circulated each month.

The same Appointments Adviser circulates a list of vacant posts each month. This list is available to all those clergy who are looking for a move and contains details of stipendiary, specialist, team rector, team vicar and house for duty vacancies which have been submitted. These details are also available on a website.

Internal moves

Perhaps the most frequent place for a change of parish to be discussed is in a meeting with a member of a diocese's senior staff. A need for such a move may also emerge from a ministerial review or 'appraisal' meeting. The senior staff – bishops, archdeacon, dean and advisers – will meet every two or three weeks and always on their agenda will be vacant parishes and clergy who are asking for a move. Following a consultation meeting with the PCC there will also be a profile of the vacant parish and a description of the kind of person they are looking for as their next vicar. It would be usual for the bishop or archdeacon to suggest a name to parish representatives after a senior staff meeting.

Private patrons

This system of making parochial appointments is unique to the Church of England and has its roots in the history and foundation of the Church. The 'living' of a parish is 'owned' by a patron. As already described, the patron of a majority of livings is the diocesan bishop, although in a significant number of parishes the living is 'owned' by colleges or trusts.

Most patrons will take great care in selecting clergy for parishes. The larger patrons, colleges and the Crown, will compile their own lists of candidates looking for a move and suggest names appropriately. The patrons who have historic endowments will also often give some financial support to clergy in their livings, on occasions make grants to repair their houses, and even offer summer schools and opportunities for clergy who occupy their living to attend in-service training events.

How long it all takes

For someone in a parochial appointment who is thinking about a move, timescale is important. An approximate estimate of how long it takes to find and arrange a move would be two years from first conversations to starting in a new parish. Of course, many people have moved in a much shorter timescale and may have been overwhelmed by the speed of it all. Congregation members as well as clergy may like to know what exactly happens and why it often seems to take so long. The process is something like this, though there will be variations between dioceses.

⇨ The present vicar signifies that they are going to leave either because they have found another job or because they have reached the age for retirement.
⇨ A vacancy occurs when the present office holder signs a Deed of Resignation with a date from which it will take effect.

➪ The Diocesan Secretary writes to the churchwardens with guidelines about what will happen during a vacancy.

➪ The Rural/Area Dean visits the PCC to talk about how the service cover and pastoral care will be organized.

➪ The Registrar or Diocesian Secretary will write to the churchwardens asking them to convene a Section 11 meeting to prepare a parish profile and statement of needs for the parish. Two parish representatives will be elected to take part in the confidential interview process of meeting candidates.

➪ The Deanery and Diocesan Pastoral Committee will advise the bishop about how a further appointment will fit into a pastoral strategy or clergy deployment plan. The Archdeacon may be asked to consult if the freehold is to be suspended and an appointment made of a priest-in-charge, part-time or house for duty person.

➪ Any combination of bishop, area bishop, suffragan bishop, archdeacon, rural dean and lay chair will meet the PCC, with the patron if there is one, to go through the parish profile and discuss what kind of person might be appointed.

➪ It may be decided to advertise. If so, material may be produced by the PCC or the diocese to be sent out with an application form. Short-listing and interview dates will be agreed.

➪ If there is no advertising the bishop's senior staff meeting may suggest names from any of the sources already mentioned for the parish representatives to consider.

➪ Once a candidate acceptable to the parish representatives, bishop and patron is identified, and the candidate wishes to proceed, then immigration and child protection checks are run.

➪ If a candidate decides not to accept the post then the process of suggesting another person begins. All this may already have taken two months or more.

➪ If all is well a date is agreed to announce the appointment.

➪ An 'ingoing works' visit is made to the parsonage house to agree what repair and redecorating work is required.

➪ A date is fixed for the Induction and Institution or Licensing.

If the time taken to consult a bishop or archdeacon is added to this, together with possible time spent visiting the Clergy Appointments Advisor, a year or more can soon unfold for candidates.

Courtesies

It is always a little difficult for a clergyperson to know who to tell about their intended move and when. I know of one person who obtained and accepted a job without telling their partner. The partner dug their heels in and refused to go, so the whole thing was off. I also know of a situation where a patron withdrew an offer after a candidate had moved in, much to the embarrassment of everyone else.

A candidate's partner and family should be involved in any discussion about a move. They will often be involved in the informal part of looking at a parish. When a job is being considered in another diocese, it is important for the home bishop to be informed. There will normally be an exchange of information between bishops about a candidate.

The present parish will need to be told about a move. This will normally take place when a date for an announcement has been agreed with the bishop and press officer. Churchwardens and parish staff would normally be told, in confidence, before the public announcement. Both parishes should make the announcement on the same Sunday. The receiving diocese is responsible for press announcements.

Feelings about the process

Many clergy have to come to terms with lowered horizons and reduced expectations as they realize what they would be considered for and what they might get. Some clergy will have been bruised by the process and feel hurt at the rejection of their application or the failure of their interview to achieve for them the appointment they wanted. Others will be overwhelmed by the range of responsibilities which they are asked to take on.

Many parishes feel frustrated by the seemingly long process before a new vicar comes. The necessary confidentiality, which can be experienced as secrecy, frustrates others. Parish representatives feel a great weight on their shoulders; if an appointment goes wrong they have a sense of guilt which can last for years.

There is a widely-held view that more openness could come into the system. More jobs than at present might be advertised. The procedure of only the two parish representatives meeting the candidate/s might be revised. In some cases interview panels are allowed. Congregations will always tend towards wanting the Free Church experience of clergy 'preaching with a view'. They would like to see and experience candidates before they are appointed. The difficulty with more openness is that a person's home parish will know that they are looking around and this may damage their ministry if no appointment is attained.

Is this the best system?

It would be a fool who suggested that this is the best possible system. That there are worse ones is no justification for keeping things as they are. What is required is a developing sense of openness about the availability of appointments. There is certainly a need for every diocese to develop a better sense of having a system of pastoral care and development for its clergy, of which the possibility of an appropriate move is a part. In the end, it is likely that we set off with many high hopes which cannot be achieved. On the way we may be distracted by the flattery and encouragement of others. Some appointments will come seemingly as a matter of chance or divine providence. We just might have been in the right place at the right time. What might be hoped for is a balance between the 'godly' intervention of holy people and aspiration tempered by realistic assessment through transparent procedures. This side of the grave it is probably best that many of us do not know how or why we came to some of our appointments.

6

Not quite real vicars?

**Michael spoke of the joys and hardships of
inner-city ministry**

Many clergy do not work full-time in the parochial ministry. Some
do this by choice, some because they can only pursue a specialist
piece of work if it has a parish with it. There are many clergy now
whose base is in the local community where they worshipped as
lay people. These also exercise a real form of ministry. Some clergy,
after their 'official' retirement or alongside a secular job, or because

their partner earns enough to maintain a family, live in the vicarage and spend some time each week and on Sundays doing work which used to be carried out by full-time paid clergy. Are all these new kinds of clergy real vicars? In this chapter we shall explore and see.

Less than full-time in the parish

Some priests have varied interests and want to spend only part of their time in a parish. The shortage of clergy sometimes now means that specialist posts are combined with parish appointments. Such 'other' jobs often come in the form of a ministry of some kind which is not based in a conventional parish. This may be as industrial chaplain, hospital chaplain, agricultural chaplain, youth chaplain or other kind of denominational specialist. These appointments can take a minister away from the local pastoral situation for a few hours or for several days per week. Most appointments of this kind are called part-time or 'dual role' and are linked with a congregation in some way. Because such appointments are becoming so frequent they need detailed consideration at this stage of our look at clergy life. Quite understandably, although students visit and hear from specialist ministers, little of the detail of this work can be taught at college.

Dual role ministers

Dual role ministers have two or more designated areas – two types of focus for their work. Usually they also work on two different physical pieces of territory. This can lead to a split-personality kind of lifestyle, where different behaviour is left behind or adopted as the minister moves from one sector to another. The very title 'dual role' suggests, gives permission for, different roles to be acted out. There might be nothing intrinsically wrong with this. It may well be the only way that some ministers can work.

The concept of 'reflective practice' is one which I want to commend so that clergy can cope with two or more jobs without having a 'breakdown'. It requires collection of data and analysis, and a spirituality which searches for the activity of God in the frantic busyness of our many different roles. For those in dual roles it gives a real opportunity for the enrichment of our spiritual traditions because we can bring many experiences of the secular world to bear on our religious life.

There is no one manual or text book which will give a definition of 'reflective practice'. It is a way of thinking and acting which can help us to become more objective about our work. It requires you to decide how you will review what you are doing. Your reasons for needing to do this will be many – you may feel there are not enough hours in the week for all your activities, you may need to re-adjust your priorities, you could sense that you are being pushed in a certain direction against your will in some areas of your work. If these issues, and some other similar ones, are significant for you then you do need to begin to think about how you approach your work.

'Reflective practice' is a way of being able to stand back. The best way for you to do this is to get a 'work consultant' of some kind. This can be someone provided by your diocese or denomination or some trained person who you invite yourself. There are also some books and training programmes available to assist with your attempts at objectivity. Most jobs in the church contain too high expectations and you will find that you have competing priorities. If you can establish the method, 'reflective practice' will help you to feel good about the work which, after negotiation, you choose to do. It will also help you to be able to say 'no' to other requests and to things which are not key to the work you are there to do.

With the aid of a diagram (Figure 6.1) we can see how things might be interrelated, how one thing is, or is not, connected to another, and how it all contributes to spiritual growth and understanding. It is a way to explore working relationships in dual role ministry.

One ministry

The writings of very many dual role ministers emphasize time and time again that they do not see themselves as having two Christian ministries but one call which is being worked out in two different situations. Oneness is important. It counters immediately the schizophrenic connotations of 'dual' in dual role ministries. It also forces us to address the question of oneness in debates about stipendiary/non-stipendiary, specialist and beneficed, ministers in secular employment and ordained members of local ministry teams. The

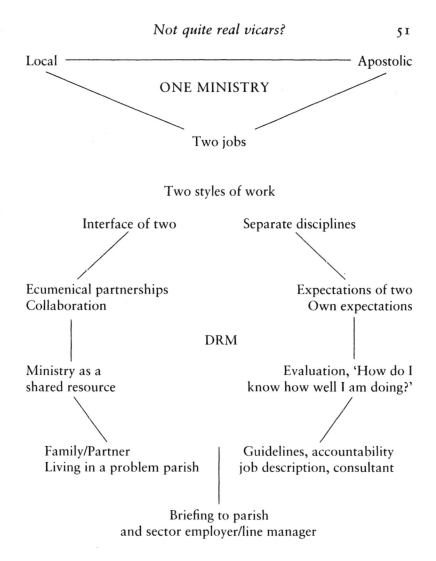

Local ————————————————————— Apostolic

ONE MINISTRY

Two jobs

Two styles of work

Interface of two   Separate disciplines

Ecumenical partnerships   Expectations of two
Collaboration   Own expectations

DRM

Ministry as a   Evaluation, 'How do I
shared resource   know how well I am doing?'

Family/Partner   Guidelines, accountability
Living in a problem parish   job description, consultant

Briefing to parish
and sector employer/line manager

Figure 6.1 Working relationships in dual role ministry

'one' in all this is the one ministry which all the people of God
share through their baptism and the oneness which we all share in
the calling we have, from God and the Church, to the Order of the
ordained within our Church and denomination.

Two jobs

The difference then is that DRMs have two jobs and working relationships. Two jobs, probably one with responsibility for a congregation and one a specialist, sector piece of work. Each has a different discipline and each makes a different set of demands. The different disciplines mean that it is better to have something about both written down. That in itself will pose a new challenge for some. Two jobs also means two sets of expectations, three if private lives and families are included. It is essential that there is a job description for each part of the job and that both parties see both parts of the description. Regular review needs to be put in place at the outset both for the working out of the job and for the integrated process of reflective practice required of the minister.

Horror stories

At an early stage in any reflection on split appointments there needs to be a recitation of the problems which often occur, some of which can be avoided. I have been involved in putting together many such appointments both in Industrial Mission and in Adult Education. In the C of E, bishops and pastoral committees see a difficult, run-down parish which is beyond pastoral reorganization as ripe for a dual role appointment. This is to be resisted at all costs.

Difficult parishes require more work, not less. It simply builds up the stress if a minister returns from the sector part of the job to an uphill task and a pile of problems which, because they are immediate and identifiable, can easily dominate a day and a week. Specialist work can be squeezed out because there you have to make your own running. No-one expects to see you; it is up to you how you fill your diary, which visits you make. But empty spaces will be gobbled up by what is seen as equally, or more tangibly, parish business.

There is a problem here for partners and families who are placed in difficult parishes. They do not necessarily go away to another environment. The pressures of living can be great, either in an urban area stacked with social problems or a deserted rural village with cautious natives who are still getting used to the new prayer book of 1662, or incomers who use the village as a dormitory and want more not less of the nostalgic rural idyll. Working relationships are really at the heart of dual role ministries. They have to be worked at. Establishing the right relationships can be very draining – and extremely time-consuming.

Integration

The very nature of dual role means that there is an opportunity for doing some integrated thinking. At its basic level, preaching about the other job and visitors from one to the other can help both to establish good cross-barrier working relationships and encourage integrated thinking. What does the constant moving from one environment to a radically different one do to a person? I can remember one sector minister saying rather disparagingly about his parish, 'Mentally I put my old clothes on when I leave the college and go back to my local church – a description which conjures up pictures of different mind-sets, different cultures and unequal responses to the two halves of a job.

Integrated thinking means that the dual role minister is working at this question of relatedness at a number of levels. It all begins with the theological assumption that there is one human person here with one call to ministry. There is one faith and one God active in revealing the kingdom in all sectors of life. We may just see the sector, secular, part of our work as invigorating and interesting. We live in a tradition which does not naturally affirm work, industry and commerce as places for spiritual growth and development. In these days, when there is so much disillusionment with work and so much insecurity in the field of employment, there is an even greater need for what Teilhard de Chardin called 'the divinisation of our activities'. This can only be attempted if we are prepared to work at these questions of how one part of our work informs another and how this thinking can be shared with others.

Working relationships

The key to success in dual role appointments, as in all other work, is the establishment of good working relationships. I am sure that the possibility of success in developing this area lies in

regular evaluation. It begins with a clear contract for both sides
of the job. It means that 'someone' has negotiated the appointment with both sides and even spoken with them. Who is this
someone? Occasionally, the appointments system in a denomination will name the responsible person. Sometimes you will
have to set up the process yourself. The recipe for disaster is
the part of our ecclesiastical culture which panders either to the
'talented individual' model, where ministers have sole responsibility to work it out for themselves, or to the 'laissez faire' model,
where the whole situation is so disturbing that nobody actually
discusses what needs to be done. 'It will all work out.' If it goes
well the denomination takes the credit. If it goes wrong then
the minister was not up to it! Agreements at the outset make
it possible for regular evaluations to take place. These can be conducted at a number of levels. I favour a short check-out after
three months and a revision of job descriptions, if necessary, after
one year. It is at this length of time that unexpressed expectations
begin to reveal themselves and conflict emerges. If an appointment
is for five years, then there needs to be a major review after four
years.

A broader vision for ordained ministry?

Looking at the practice of ministry and going on this excursion
into dual role appointments have revealed something of the changing nature of the expectations placed on ordained ministers and
how these expectations relate to new relationships with lay people
and congregations. The position of those in ordained ministry has
changed already. Worker and non-stipendiary ministers have been
saying this to the Church for at least 50 years now. It is these sector
ministers who can make profound theological reflections as well as
give practical advice on this new but established feature of practice
within the ordained ministry. They have more experience in this
than anyone else. Equally, they are the unheard group within the
ranks of the ordained. They are neither fully committed parish
ministers nor totally absorbed specialist or worker priests. It is
hard to find time for chapter meetings and fraternals; synods are
irrelevant unless you are the speaker. Yet clergy with licences, those
with dual role jobs, those in secular employment and those in house
for duty posts make up a significant proportion of the ordained

people within our denominations. Your presence already reflects a changed church.

Local ministry

Variations on conventional patterns of parochial ministry lead to a discussion of local ministry. It is becoming clear that a change is taking place across our principal denominations away from the more traditional, clerically based, professional, full-time stipendiary ministry towards a way of understanding the local church and its congregation which expects its lay members to recognize and want to use their varied gifts in the service of God by giving their time and 'ministries' to their local church. A key element in this developing situation is that clergy and laity *together* are becoming committed to working in partnership on the many tasks – prayer, worship, education, pastoral care, evangelism, preparation for baptism or confirmation – which characterize the life of the local church, many of which would previously have been the province of the minister.

So, what is the exact understanding of this new concept which has developed and which is called local ministry? Robin Greenwood, who has written in most helpful ways on this subject, makes a comment which is central to our theme: 'Local can be summarised in two ways. First it is a unit that is able to sustain and work with a visible team of people. Second it is the scale on which it is possible for people to relate person to person.'

If that is a little too abstract and impersonal, local ministry has developed in a number of Anglican dioceses and has a much more familiar face. In such places, which may be either one parish or a group of parishes, lay people are called out by their local congregations to perform certain pastoral, priestly and organizational tasks. The diocese or other Christian unit agrees to share in the selection of such local ministers and to provide support and training. In some dioceses members of the local ministry group call out one person to be ordained as a priest and exercise a ministry only within that particular group of parishes; this person is called a Local Non-Stipendiary Minister (LNSM).

What is important, and a key development for the future, is the constitution and make-up of local ministry teams. Most interestingly, it is not just those involved who are commissioned in this local ministry: it is the whole congregation. Everyone shares in the commission and the work that is being done. Local ministry is in the most definite sense both *shared* and *collaborative*. The concept of ordained and lay people choosing to work together in new and innovative ways is integral to this ministry. Undoubtedly it demands both trust and confidence in one another from all involved. It certainly reflects an excitement about a vision of what can be achieved in a local community through this new kind of partnership.

Experience assessed

Sufficient local ministry projects exist for a first stock-taking to be done. At a consultation for those involved in local ministry teams, organized by the Edward King Institute for Ministry Development, two fundamental and commonly held beliefs were acknowledged and shared by those present:

- the belief that through baptism God calls each person to ministry;
- the belief that God gives to the Church the gifts that it needs to be the Church in a particular place.

Many of those at the consultation spoke of the excitement of engaging in the work and the joy of being trusted and valued by their local churches. Here are groups of people trained and authorized to extend the love of God into their local communities through special tasks and roles. Work is organized, supported and evaluated. It does not create an 'elite' who have superior positions in a congregation. It is a recognition of how the skills and abilities already present within the members of a congregation can be harnessed and focused to increase the effectiveness of what a local church is trying to do. It is an acting out of what is seen as a new call from God for our time.

House for duty appointments

Among the newest forms of locally-based parish work for the ordained are house for duty appointments. In these a clergyperson occupies a parsonage house, free of rent and rates, on the same basis as stipendiary clergy but gives up to three days and Sunday for ministry in exchange.

Some of those who take up these appointments are retired but want to continue in active parochial ministry until their seventieth birthday. There are other clergy, who perhaps have been non-stipendiary and retired early, who want to offer themselves without payment in this way. Again, there are others who are free to make this offer because their partner is earning well. There are a few clergy who have an income from part-time private work and can keep themselves while also exercising this ministry.

There can be no doubt that this arrangement has all the potential to be very stressful indeed. Its worst aspect is that the parish can think that it still has a full-time vicar in all but name. Many people, often from the wider community, still regard the house for duty person as a full-time vicar. Some from the congregation will do the same. Some of those appointed will in practice give far more than three days. Critics say that this kind of appointment props up an already unviable system and gives dioceses the opportunity to avoid more difficult pastoral reorganization.

A positive collaborative experiment

In many situations house for duty appointments have been experienced as a very good thing. Deployment of what is in effect a volunteer requires that the neighbouring priest becomes priest-in-charge. If this arrangement arises from an existing situation of collaborative practice, then there is an enriching of ministry, a positive exchange of skills and a real interchange of congregation members across boundaries.

The searching questions that arise from these clerical appointments are for dioceses. If house for duty is a part of a definite plan which a deanery has negotiated, then it can be one of the new patterns of ministry for the future. Where such schemes have been well thought through, duties can be divided, co-operation understood and a larger working unit established. There are even greater benefits if several parishes and clergy are involved. The appointment then becomes an ingredient in a much wider team or group.

Changed leadership styles

All of the styles of ministry described in this chapter point towards significant learnings about appropriate leadership styles in situations other than one person/one parish. There is no doubt at all that in England this will be the pattern of ministry for the future. In many places it is already happening, and with some success. The new task of the clergyperson as leader is to make collegiality of activity possible for those engaged in the life of a congregation and then for those within the ministry team.

Ministry in transition

None of the new words used to describe new ministries (house for duty, NSM, etc.) fits easily with clergy and lay people as they move from a traditional and inherited situation towards a new era which seems less secure. Traditional patterns of leadership will not bring these new parochial patterns into being. Words like team and group and cluster still arouse great hostility in many ecclesiastical circles. I have even heard the hurtful remark that Anglican clergy working in this way are introducing the Methodist Circuit system under another name. I prefer to point to many other places in the Anglican Communion where clergy have always been thin on the ground, but where the growth in congregation numbers is significant. In our close European neighbour, France, important examples of missionary outreach began over 60 years ago. One of those missionary pioneers, Cardinal Suenens, wrote, 'A true leader will find his place when he has succeeded in helping others to find theirs.' That remark could be the motto or benchmark for clergy who are committed to new ways of working. The practice of ministry for the future will be *collaborative*; it will be *varied* in how it understands and uses the ordained; and it will be *local* as clergy and lay people in groups or 'clusters' of congregations walk out together in faith to search for the type of local church which God calls us all to discover.

7

Goodbye and hello

And then, one Lent, Basil simply gave up

There is a very human side to leaving a job of any kind. There will
be the inevitable uncertainties about whether you have done the
right thing. Just occasionally there is a mutual sigh of relief if the
job has been a bad fit and both sides are sure that an ending is
best. Much more often a sense of excitement about the new is
balanced by the sadness of leaving work colleagues and friends
who have been an essential and intimate part of the context and
development of one large part of life. There is and should be an
appropriate anxiety about moving on. The old and familiar ways
and work routine have given a sense of order and security and now
that is coming to an abrupt end. Is this the right move? Will all
the necessary skills be there for the new work to be done? What
if some of the new personalities turn out to be more awkward than

anticipated? Can I live up to the challenge? Do I have real skills and gifts to offer, will I continue to grow and develop – or will they see more of my frailties than my strengths? How much will I live under the shadow of the person who was there before me? If I have a family, how will they settle? One thing is sure and inevitable, there is a certain stage beyond which there is no going back.

How to decide when to leave

There is rarely a completely right time to leave. Nor is there a completely right decision about the best work to go on to. There can be advice from friends and work colleagues, but there can never be wholly good or bad advice. What people say comes as part of the evidence on which your decision is made. Some advice brings positive 'vibes', other is unwelcome; some advice is sycophantic, or unrealistic about your actual possibilities. On occasions, if the advice is optimistically realistic, the goal can still be unobtainable. Advice is like a mirror, it shows you up in a number of different lights. Only you will know how you react to different pieces of advice. The balance of what is said and offered contributes to the decision you will make. That decision is informed both by your inner feelings, spirituality and journey and by the practicalities of what has to be done next and the human needs of yourself, your family and the others with whom you work.

Professionally, the most difficult side of leaving is both personal and practical. In parish life, though not only there, your work has been built on a whole series of personal relationships. Pastoral work brings clergy an intimacy with individuals and families in a whole range of situations which is open to few others. This whole series of trusting relationships is severed when 'their vicar' anounces a move to the next job. All clergy feel that in some sense they have betrayed that trust when their departure is announced – and so they should. That sense of moving away and severance needs to be explored.

As well as the very real sense of let-down when a friend goes, many parish pastoral relationships verge on dependency. Some people value and use the care of their clergy but do not move on; we have all known, and sat with, people who tell us the same story again and again. We also have to look at ourselves and our emotions, because we need secure relationships as well. We need to recognize how much our pastoral work meets our own needs as well as those of the people we visit – we too can be dependent. Equally, we need to recognize that other clergy will reach different people in the same parish; we are not what everyone is looking for! All of these very human, personal aspects which address our fragility need to be visited as we conclude that it is time to move on.

Managing the move

As a result of many years of working with people in transition from one place to another, a very useful grid has been developed which gives a series of ways of thinking about a move and compartmentalizing the different mental processes which have to go on.

> ⇨ What do I leave behind?
> ⇨ What do I take with me?
> ⇨ What do I need to know?

What do I leave behind?

Quite clearly what is left behind is almost everything that has formed the old job. We leave behind house, garden, church, churchyard, church hall, local pubs, clubs and restaurants – no more visits to the familiar chip shop or take-away. All these physical things go with the finality of the removal van. Human things also go. The old relationship with all the people known and worked with is lost for ever. The congregation(s) no longer have you as their vicar. The community groups, the pensioners clubs and even the youth club or group will no longer have you as their supporter, encourager and pastor. Gone also are the sights, sounds and smells of the place which has known you for however many years.

There are some essentials to leave behind, or destroy:

- The files must be pruned to the essentials, giving appropriate attention to the Data Protection Act which determines access to files.
- The Child Protection papers must be checked through with the appointed representatives and then stored in a secure place.
- The parish computer database must be handed over to someone, with instructions on how to access it.

- Any paper record cards about pastoral work must be destroyed, kept in a safe place for your successor or, in rare cases, come with you.
- All papers regarding the church building must be given to the church officers or the building committee.
- Someone has to know where the churchyard grave plan is kept.
- Historic papers relating to the church and parish must be returned to the church safe or given to the Diocesan Records and Registers Officer.
- A list of faults in the vicarage or repairs needed must be left in the house or with the Diocesan Property Officer.

What do I take with me?

Things that come with you can be personal and internal as well as practical. The place in which you have worked and the role you had there contribute in a significant way towards the formation of the person you are. At the time of a move enormous changes take place. The context of the former parish and its wider community has given you identity and security, and that will be left behind; but you will still be you. The person you are is what the former place has made you, scars and all, and this can be an appropriate, and inescapable, time to begin to reflect on who you are. You may be leaving because you never felt completely at home or content and you will have regrets and hopes as you go. All these feelings will also be true for partner and children – some of them will be true even for pets!

Most importantly, you take with you the things which are not tied to that place, skills which have been developed and refined and will now get new application. If your move is part of your personal development you may have chosen the new job in order to bring unused or latent skills and interests to the new place.

It might be good to list your hopes and the skills you bring at the time of the move and then to re-visit this after a year to review how the transition has been.

You might also want to list any regrets and feelings of guilt and bereavement when you leave and visit these in your reflections to see how you are dealing with them.

What do I need to know?

There are some key things which you will need to know as you arrive in the new place.

- Is there a job description or something in the parish profile which sets out the expectations of the person appointed to this job?
- How did the last person leave? Were there troubles, and will there be practical and human repercussions of this in your first months?
- Did the bishop, archdeacon or denominational leader give you any indication of what might be expected of you in this new post? Do you need any training in order to do parts of the new job? If there are colleagues, how do they feel about the appointment? Did they all agree with the decision to appoint you?
- Is there a community or civic expectation that you will take on any public roles? Can community leaders or council officials brief you on these?
- What is the level of ecumenical co-operation?
- Who is holding tasks until you arrive – and should you take them on? How will you negotiate the gap between practical expectations and what you are prepared or able to do?

Leaving well

There is an art in leaving a job which comes with practice and experience. Because it is a time so charged with emotion, I have never felt that I got it right. Some clergy are tempted to say what they think about the place in a last sermon or 'position paper'. There is a delicate balance between 'speaking the truth in love' as you go and either being too bland or causing offence. It is important to keep church officers briefed about how you are going to leave and what handover arrangements you are making. It is equally important to keep on talking to partner and family about the consequences of the move.

I have a particular hobby-horse about closing down activities whose life has ended. We all want to leave with the hope that those in the previous place have good feelings about us. However, if we have failed to tackle some significant issues then all we are doing is ensuring that our successor arrives with an even bigger bundle of problems to confront! If there are some activities which have run their course it is almost a responsibility on you to see that they are ended before you go. This may make you unpopular at the time with some people. It may mean that you take the blame for closing whatever it is down. This burden is better placed on you than on your successor in the first months of their work.

A stage in your personal journey

There are cascading thoughts about a move. Will I be able to do the job? Did I make the right decision? Will my partner resent leaving their job and will they get another one? Will the children settle in the new school and will their education be damaged? Clergy who move parish jobs have to take on larger family responsibilities than a person who does not have to relocate with a change of job. The house move, in a 'tied house' situation, is never easy and different dioceses and denominations offer different levels of support around a move. There is a considerable financial cost as well as a personal one in any physical move. Stress levels do go up and only some of them can be contained and managed. The unpredictable has a cunning way of catching us unawares.

There is another human aspect to changing jobs. This move may not be the one you hoped for. All moves are a mixture of the need to achieve and feel fulfilled, frustration with where you are now, and the need to be refreshed. There is a scaling-up and a scaling-down of hopes and (if it can be said of ecclesiastical appointments) ambition at different stages of life. Moves from a curacy to a first parish contain one whole bundle of thoughts. Changing the size of a parish is always a challenge. A move from inner-city to suburban or rural requires new skills and often massive adjustments in lifestyle. The job change in mid or late career begins to define the level at which the whole ministry has been conducted. The move to retirement, while bringing opportunities hoped for by many, is a change which takes away much of the support in public life for who you have been.

Person and role

Who am I in all this? Every sensitive person reflects often on the balance between the person they think they are and the person they have to be in order to do the job and carry out some of its public roles. Job changes are a pivotal time in this reflection, an opportunity to adjust the job to the shape of person you would like to be. This is an important aspect of a job change; it is also a luxury not open to many of the population of this world. We should treat the opportunity to move as a privilege. Being too self-centred about a move is a great danger; have we have looked most at our own needs in making this decision?

Leaving also requires sensitivity to the needs of the church you have promised to serve. There may be occasions when you decide to leave, even if you do not want to, because the parish and congregation will benefit from a new approach. There are other jobs which anyone might feel called to do simply because they need to be done. Clergy moves are not all about personal gratification; they also need to take into consideration the needs of the church and the tasks which have to be done.

Legions of people have been surprised at how much a sense of calling has been fulfilled in a job which would never have occurred to them but was suggested by a church leader or at the invitation of a congregation. We shall never know in this life how much of a hand God's innovative Spirit has had in the way our moves have been made. There is a pearl of great price for the Christian, and for much of life it will feel like an irritating grain of sand. I cannot be all that I want to be in this life, but I can try to become who God wants me to be. Each of us can only attempt to fulfil our vocation wherever we find ourselves, by developing our Christian ministry in ways where talent and opportunity can come as close together as chance and planning will allow.

Note: Ways of signifying readiness for a move are dealt with in other sections. The names of private patrons and the Archbishops' Appointments Adviser can be found in *The Church of England Yearbook*, produced annually by Church House Publishing.

8

Glittering prizes

**The bishop spent most of his time in the parishes,
encouraging his clergy and their people**

There is a common saying about the reform of infant baptism
practices: we are in the main unhappy with the way things are done
now, but all proposals for reform are worse. Much the same
can be said of the way in which senior appointments are made in
the Church of England. I cannot speak for any other denomination. This chapter will look at what possibilities there are for

'promotion'. Any look at the ministry which clergy undertake has to consider the preferment, or career, structure.

Ambition is not an approved thing within clerical circles, nor should it be. A naked desire to get jobs or to be offered senior positions is distasteful in any profession. However, it is completely appropriate for anyone to feel a sense of wellbeing or achievement in the work they undertake. It is also appropriate for others to recognize ability or good work done and suggest more responsibility.

A system of preferment by recommendation has an air of old-fashioned quaintness about it. In an age when open advertising is the order of the day, the opportunity for favouritism or corruption is great. Within the parochial system of the Church of England appointments are made to parishes by what is called patronage. In this situation a bishop, a private individual, a university, a trust or the Crown can recommend names for freehold livings. Appointments to senior positions are hardly ever advertised; bishoprics are never advertised; deaneries and archdeaconries only rarely. Cathedral canonries are normally only advertised if they have a specialist diocesan appointment linked with them. Rural deans are appointed by the diocesan bishop.

Is the system fair enough?

I have been the member of a senior staff team for more than eight years so have experienced much of the system by which clergy are appointed to parishes. Two of my previous jobs were as the senior person in a specialist diocesan ministry, where I experienced many of the ways in which most clergy will move posts. I have also lived on the edge of the senior appointments system. I can say that I have seen a gradual opening up of many parochial appointments to competitive interview as is the case with all specialist appointments. I cannot say that in any way have I seen moves put in place to create a similar system of open access in senior appointments. It is the place where the patronage of those in the most senior circles of the Church of England is still very influential.

As a reaction to experienced partiality in appointments under Archbishop Robert Runcie, the Revd Dr Garry Bennett produced the, at first, anonymous preface to *Crockfords Clerical Directory* in which he instanced the way in which those close to the Archbishop in different phases of his life had been given promotion. It is my view that under the ten-year episcopate of Archbishop George Carey a similar trawl through Crockfords and a look at church party allegiance could show an even more pronounced partiality among senior appointments. The difficulty with such a use of the system is that there are long-term consequences for the Church of England. It will take two generations before balance can be restored among diocesan and suffragan bishops.

Senior glittering prizes: bishops

There is a mystery about senior appointments which those involved would call a necessary process of confidentiality. Consultation at many levels does go on within the Church to identify those who might be considered for senior appointments. The weakness in the system is that the people or 'candidates' themselves do not know that they are being considered and consequently have no opportunity to verify the information which is being gathered about them.

It is in the making of senior appointments that representatives of the Archbishops, the Prime Minister and the Crown come into their own. Those inside the system, and those outside it who are interested, become acutely aware of the strength of 'the establishment' and the power and influence of the Crown and, potentially, of the Prime Minister in the making of senior appointments. Much manoeuvring and positioning is charted with amusing accuracy by the Victorian novelist Anthony Trollope. History books also record the political influence of Victorian Prime Ministers like Palmerston and Gladstone. There is considerable evidence that Winston Churchill had strong views about the successor to Archbishop William Temple and that he 'blocked' Bishop George Bell because he had criticized the policy of indiscriminate bombing of German towns towards the end of the war. Rumour has it that Mrs Thatcher had her own views about a successor to Archbishop Robert Runcie, but any further speculation on that matter would be singularly inappropriate! Our new Archbishop of Canterbury, Dr Rowan Williams, has made interesting comments about the public debate over his election. He says that the media contacted him daily and details of his life and opinions were a subject of public debate. At the same time, no-one from the Crown Appointments Commission was allowed to contact him and he had no opportunity to clarify his details and opinions with those who would actually make the appointment.

How the system works

Every diocese has to elect a Vacancy in See Committee, which remains dormant until a diocesan bishop announces his retirement. This committee then comes into its own with a burst of activity. It is convened to meet the Prime Minister's Appointments Secretary and the Archbishops' Appointments Secretary. It produces a written profile of the diocese and a statement of needs describing the attributes needed in a new diocesan bishop. The committee elects four of its number to join the Crown Appointments Commission.

The two Appointments Secretaries visit a diocese where a vacancy is about to occur and, over a period of two days, meet a wide range of people from the church, civic and secular communities. They then produce their own report on the diocese for the Crown Appointments Commission.

Once all this consulting and report writing is complete, the Commission, made up of the two archbishops, four people from the diocesan Vacancy in See Committee, six from the General Synod and the two secretaries, goes off to a secret location to consider names. Two preferred names, in order, go to the Prime Minister who he chooses one or the other, or asks for more names. Only at this late stage will the unsuspecting candidate be made aware of his candidacy. If he is willing to accept, the name goes to the Crown for approval and an offer can be made.

I have been a part of this 'secret' process for my own diocese. I would say that if we have to use this system, it works well. I would also support those who say that a greater amount of information should be given to the members of the Commission about each of the suggested names. More than that, I would want those whose profiles are being collected by the Appointments Secretaries to have an opportuntity to check their file and to be able to add information and references for any part of their life which they consider has not been given adequate coverage.

After the national process of selection is completed, local activities begin. There is a process by which the person nominated becomes the bishop of the diocese. In what most people see as an anachronism, the college of canons of the cathedral of the diocese has to elect the person – after his name has been announced! This election is then confirmed by a ceremony in the cathedral of the province (Canterbury or York), after which the bishop can take up his new office. If he is not already a bishop, he moves on to a service of consecration and then makes homage to the sovereign. At this point the temporalities (properties and the right of patronage to livings in the gift of the bishop) are restored and there can then be a service of enthronement or installation in what will become his cathedral.

What is the job of a bishop?

Bishops cannot win. They are the focus of great attention from clergy and parishioners and have tremendous expectations placed upon them. They receive massive projections of both praise for work which others do and blame when what is expected or hoped for cannot be delivered.

More than anything else, the job of a bishop in the Church is one of privilege. It carries a great inheritance of power and public position in ways that most other professions have lost in their leadership. To be a bishop is automatically to become a public figure, offered opportunities greater than any one person can take up or fulfil. It is a position open to great abuse of power because there are almost no accountability checks. The job requires a super-human amount of ability and humility. Bishops and their families pay a heavy price for high office.

Much training and support is given to bishops, especially when they come into office – the archbishops have a full-time training officer. All bishops (and their wives) are in supportive cells; they meet regularly in sub-regional groupings and frequently as a House of Bishops with the Archbishops. My own limited work with new bishops, and with those involved in their appointment and training, has led to a diagram (Figure 8.1) which describes the internal church-facing and the external world-facing work of a bishop.

Area and suffragan bishops

All bishops are bishops and are consecrated in the same way. As such, they belong to one of the three Orders of bishops, priests and deacons in the catholic or universal Church. In their work bishops have different roles and responsibilities. Diocesan bishops have the whole of a diocese as their responsibility. Suffragan bishops come in two kinds, with or without a territorial area of responsibility, but both are assistants sharing pastoral responsibility devolved from the

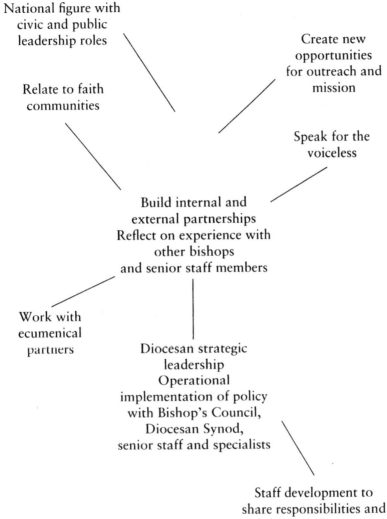

National figure with
civic and public
leadership roles

Relate to faith
communities

Create new
opportunities
for outreach and
mission

Speak for the
voiceless

Build internal and
external partnerships
Reflect on experience with
other bishops
and senior staff members

Work with
ecumenical
partners

Diocesan strategic
leadership
Operational
implementation of policy
with Bishop's Council,
Diocesan Synod,
senior staff and specialists

Staff development to
share responsibilities and
produce the next
generation of leaders

Figure 8.1 The work of a bishop

oversight of a diocesan bishop. Area bishops have a certain amount of independent responsibility given to them by the bishop of the diocese for one part of his diocese, often made up of one or more archdeaconries. Suffragan bishops without area responsibilities often have specialist work which they do in their own right, or supervise, while sharing in other episcopal duties across a diocese. Assistant bishops are often retired bishops or bishops who have returned from overseas. They have a licence to carry out whatever duties the diocesan bishop requests of them.

Can we re-invent bishops?

We are at a stage in the life of the Church of England when there is considerable disquiet about the way in which bishops are chosen. We also live in a church and wider community which is beginning to question the hierarchical assumptions of a generation of bishops, as well as their inherited lifestyle.

In 2001 Baroness Perry of Southwark, for the General Synod and the Archbishops' Council, published a report called *Working with the Spirit: choosing diocesan bishops* (also known as the Perry Report). A quotation from that report describes the current appointments dilemma very well:

> Suffragan bishops are appointed by diocesan bishops. The appointment is usually made after consultation . . . but diocesan bishops differ as to the degree to which they consult and the extent to which their decision is affected by the views of others. . . . If a significant proportion of the pool of candidates consisted of suffragans similar to the diocesans who appointed them, this could produce a 'cloning' effect . . . Thus 90% of those who become diocesan bishops are selected, largely on the basis of a reference from a diocesan bishop, from a pool chosen by diocesan bishops. (page 18, para 2.9)

The work of a bishop

So, what does a bishop do? The Church of England is episcopally led and synodically governed, the Bishop of Durham's report *Working as One Body* tells us. The nature of that episcopal leadership covers the internal workings of the Church from parish level to diocesan and on to national levels. It also involves a kind of moral or community leadership which derives from the opportunities which bishops have through their inherited role in public life.

Professor Anthony Mellows, Emeritus Professor of Law at King's College, London, was chairman of a group which produced a report for the General Synod and Archbishops' Council on the work and working conditions of bishops. This report, called *Resourcing Bishops* and known as the Mellows Report, was published in 2001. The Mellows Report says that

> the bishop's vocation [is] to be a focus and an enabler of unity. It is a vocation that is complex, reflecting the nature of unity itself . . . The truth is that the bishop is rooted in, and belongs to, his diocese; but he also belongs to the universal Church, which he represents to the local church. (page 18, par 2.4.6)

The Perry Report, in its introduction, says that 'The role of . . . bishops is an onerous one and those who are called to serve in this way must be capable of exercising great responsibility.' There is little sense of having a 'glittering prize' among those who are called to become bishops. On the contrary, there is a very great sense of obligation and responsibility summed up in that phrase of Baroness Perry's that all those who are chosen to become bishops are 'called to serve'.

The lesser glittering prizes: Deans

Deans rank second to diocesan bishops in the hierarchy of a diocese. It is probably fair to say that the work of deans has changed more than any other among senior churchpeople in the past 50 years. This is because the work of cathedrals has changed and the task of maintaining cathedrals has become a major business enterprise.

Deans are appointed by the Crown after consultation with the diocese concerned, the archbishops and the appointments secretaries. In a very few cases, such as Sheffield and Bradford, deans are appointed by private patrons who have retained patronage from the time when a cathedral was a parish church.

The senior staff meeting of a diocese always includes the dean. He or she also has a civic ministry of their own and, like the cathedral itself, a role in the diocese which is independent of the bishop and his staff.

The work of cathedrals, with inevitable consequences for deans, has been reviewed by a group chaired by Lady Howe of Aberavon. This work was commissioned by the two archbishops in response to a growing sense that the statutes by which they were administered needed reviewing. Cathedrals are guardians of a great heritage, they employ many clergy and specialist lay people, they attract hundreds of thousands of tourists each year and cost millions of pounds to maintain. In the report published in 1994 called *Heritage and Renewal* Lady Howe's group suggested a revision of the management structures within cathedrals, gave an important new place to the bishop on behalf of the diocese and affirmed the place of cathedrals in the mission of the Church and the life of the nation.

Deans are much more than general managers of the vast enterprise which is a cathedral. They are frequently accomplished people in their own right and have much to give to the public life and culture of a nation. More than ever, they have to be team players with the canons who form the chapter and the lay people who administer the building.

Canons

The legislation which followed the publication of *Heritage and Renewal* is called the Cathedrals Measure 1999. It allows for the establishment of a college of canons. This consists of the dean, the suffragan bishops, full-time assistant bishops and archdeacons of the diocese, and the canons of the cathedral. It is this group who form the spiritual, theological and pastoral heart of the life of a cathedral. The Measure also requires the constitution of every cathedral to provide for the appointment of lay canons.

Residentiary canons may be full-time and appointed either by the Crown or the diocesan bishop. Part-time residentiary canons will be appointed by the bishop, often in consultation with a group responsible for specialist work in a diocese. Such canons will also hold a specialist ministry post in the diocese.

Honorary and lay canons are appointed by the diocesan bishop after consultation with the chapter and his senior staff. Such appointments carry no stipend and no other responsibility than to form the Greater Chapter and advise the bishop and the dean on matters of spiritual or pastoral concern in the diocese. Those appointed as honorary canons or lay canons have often given distinguished service in the diocese or community or they have specialist or senior parish responsibilities in the diocese or beyond.

Archdeacons

Archdeacons are appointed by diocesan bishops after consultation within their diocese and with the Appointments Advisers. It is now recommended within the process for senior appointments that job descriptions are drawn up before candidates for archdeacon are considered. In practice, the work of oversight in a diocese will be determined by the diocesan bishop. The consequences of this devolution of responsibilities, or otherwise, will shape much of the work of an archdeacon.

While they are bishop's officers, archdeacons have areas of work which come to them in their own right. Much of their work and duties is set out in chapter 11, 'The archdeacon says'. They are legal officers, exercising consistory court responsibilities given to them by the Chancellor of the diocese. They have ex officio places on many diocesan committees, particularly those such as Pastoral Committees, Property Committees, Boards of Finance and Bishop's Councils which every diocese must have. They have important work in developing pastoral strategies and recruiting for parochial appointments on behalf of the bishop. Many archdeacons will chair one or more of the significant committees in the diocese which provide supervision of specialist work. The appointment of an archdeacon is a freehold one in its own right. Some archdeacons also have parochial responsibilities.

Rural and area deans

No area within the Church has undergone more revision in status than the deanery. Deanery synods were created by the Synodical Government Measure 1969. Among their tasks is

to bring together the views of the parishes of the deanery, to discuss and formulate common policies on those problems, to foster a sense of community and interdependence among those parishes, and generally to promote in the deanery the whole mission of the Church, pastoral, evangelistic, social and ecumenical.

This list also describes very well the work of the rural or area dean.

Rural or area deans are appointed by the diocesan bishop, usually after consultation by post with the clergy of the deanery. When the place of the deanery in the life of the Church appeared to be in decline, the work of the rural or area dean continued to grow. They convene the chapter meeting of clergy; with the other sequestrators they are responsible for the order and maintenance of services in a parish during a vacancy. They chair the deanery synod and work with the lay chair and standing committee in the conduct of its business. They chair the Deanery Pastoral Committee.

At a time when deaneries were being reviewed by Lord Bridge, with a certain sense of their demise, a turn-around in their fortunes took place. The Bridge Report of 1997, *Synodical Government in the Church of England: A review*, was published just when many dioceses saw an increasing need for some of their central work to be devolved. Most dioceses ask deaneries to advise on pastoral matters and on the parish share or quota. Rural or area deans are central to this work. In many dioceses specialist work is done in deaneries, sometimes with funding managed at this level.

Rural or area deans are appointed for five years. Most get some extra financial support from the diocese to enable them to pay for additional secretarial assistance. Increasingly, the work of a rural or area dean is in collaboration with the Standing and Pastoral Committees. Such collaboration is a model for similar styles of work in parishes.

9

Last jobs and retirement

Clergy about to retire are given essential re-training

Most of us reach an age which tells us that some parts of life are over. A pivotal time comes in our late fifties or very early sixties. We realize that this is our last job. Many people younger than us are taking on the tasks that we once did. They are doing them in different ways, using methods and technologies which we find less easy to comprehend. Sometimes we feel that we belong to a church which is very far from the one which called us and recognized our early vocation.

The prospect of retirement is a time when the potential for a downward spiral of feelings needs to be addressed. Yes, we know now where we ended up in the preferment stakes. We are fully aware of the privileges which have come with many jobs and through the series of personal and pastoral relationships which a life in the ordained ministry brings. Of course there are regrets. Some of these will be about the jobs we did not get. Others, perhaps more appropriately, will be about the opportunities we did not take, the battles to move a congregation forward which we avoided or the pastoral work which was left undone.

The other side of regret is a maturity of perspective. We know our limitations. We know what we learned when things went wrong. We have come to know how best we can share the gospel. We know that we shall never convert the world. There is also a deeply felt sense that our spirituality has brought us to a certain place. The times of doubt or depression brought on by tiredness and exhaustion now bear their fruit in a trusting and reflective relationship with God. How many older people – yes, a word we can now use about ourselves – say, 'I may believe less than I used to do, but what I believe I treasure more deeply'?

First preparations

This is the time to begin to think that your next move will be to retirement. It is an appropriate time to begin to think about where your retirement home will be. A long series of conversations with your partner, your family if you have one, and your friends is important. This may take the form of a whole series of anecdotes and jokes about retirement. It is not an easy subject to get into. People may feel uneasy about entering into this discussion with you. Many parishioners will not want to talk to you about this because they will begin to feel the loss of another trusted friend and pastor. They may also feel that, once you have started out on this exploration, your energy and commitment to developing the parish and congregation will be lessened.

Much more important for you will be the sense of personal adjustment. This is a time of deep and grave acceptance. This is who I am. I am not going to be discovered and catapulted to some other greater sphere of work, even if I wanted to be. This adjustment is not only in the head, it is in the heart and in the 'bowels'. To come to know this is a hard thing to accept. Jokes are one way of gradually getting it into the system. 'I am looking forward to my pensioner's passes, we will really travel with all those concessions.'

You may feel disappointed with where you have reached. There are ways of coming to this acceptance and your spiritual director or personal consultant will be a key interpreter.

The other side of the sense of disappointment may well be a great sense of relief. There is no longer the need to keep on preparing for 'something else'. The struggles and anxieties about being thought about or remembered when vacancies are coming up will be over. You may even be a little less anxious about your children and even be beginning to enjoy the times you share with your grandchildren and extended family. The sometimes very well-constructed barriers of always being a clergyperson and a little different may be beginning to melt. Priesthood always remains and will move into a new phase of self-giving. The springboard to this will be the enforced realization that we are mortal, just like all those we have ministered to over the years. In this crucial phase of approaching retirement we will need to accept the help and advice of others in ways that we have not needed in our necessarily protected, paid, housed and secure years of ministry.

The choices you have

As in every other part of your ministry, you will find that you now have more choices and opportunities than you could have imagined. Of course, this stage in your life has within it a more significant series of endings. Some of these will be around the death of trusted colleagues and friends. Those who were the models for your ministry will no longer be around. What they wrote or said, though still full of weight for you, may appear dated and you will need to revisit those memories and, as you reflect on current world and church situations, quarry what will fuel you for the next part of life's journey.

Before you move into the practical choices about retirement, go to the question about vocation. What kind of Christian is God calling you to become in this next phase of your life? Take time to mull this over. Look at some of the things you can change and come to terms more effectively with those few things about yourself you think that you cannot change. Look at how you reflect and learn. Consider in a more humble way who there is around you to help you adjust. Remember that there are others, not least your partner, who will also be anxious about these changes in your life.

Perhaps this is the time to realize more profoundly that you are only a part of the debate and that a thoughtful and prayerful dialogue with others may well bring you into a series of richer relationships. These may come because, sometimes for the first time in years (in public at least), you will have shown some vulnerability.

Practical choices

Do you have to retire, can you afford to retire, where will we live, how much will the pension be, what can our savings buy us? All these questions will crowd into your mind. There may also be an unsettling question for the more sensitive. You may have joined in many discussions over the years about old so-and-so who has stayed on for too long. You may have said that about some bishops and many of your colleagues. Are people now saying the same about you behind your back?

There is a convention that clergy rarely retire into the parish where they have had their last charge. Their presence will make the work of a new person less easy. Many congregation members will cling to you as their pastor and sometimes you may be tempted to feel that you need them around you. When the new vicar starts to bring about changes, you may feel envy or regret that you did not think of them. You may feel that he or she can get things done in weeks that you failed to achieve in years. Worst of all, you may become a power base around which the disenchanted gather to fuel and organize their resistance to the developments of the new vicar.

You now have a number of choices to consider:

- **It may be appropriate for you to move to a new job for your last five years.** In saying this I am not suggesting a 'light duty' parish. Such places hardly exist. When I was an industrial chaplain in the coal industry of South Yorkshire I saw a constructive solution offered for miners who could no longer do the heavy underground work. They became 'parent craftsmen', doing specially described jobs on the surface. These were not contrived jobs but real pieces of work or supervision which an experienced miner could do. In the work I have now, there have been a number of occasions when I have asked an experienced clergyperson to move and do a focused piece of work for five years. No-one could accuse them of empire building or making a career move. What they could do was use their experience to untie a knot or move a difficult situation forward. These were highly regarded moves. I commend the idea, not least to give some clergy a real sense of achievement through experience in their last post.

- **If you are to stay on in the same job, you still need to keep fresh.** To be a person who would really rather be somewhere else is a sad situation. There are clergy who do not want to go on to full retirement age. Many, almost all, of our professional contemporaries take early retirement. Some retire in their early or mid fifties and begin another career. That opportunity is not open to clergy in good health. The Church of England Pensions Board does not have a scheme to allow early retirement. They have done their sums and know what it would cost to have more people in their pension fund for even longer. They will do a calculation and offer to receive payments from any diocese as a lump sum to make up the contributions to retirement age, but few or no dioceses will make that quite large payment. Early retirement comes only on health grounds, and with reduced benefits.

- **Keeping fresh requires some re-invention or rediscovery of ministry** for a final few years. These are not a run-down to retirement but a re-assembling of experience, a harvesting, so that pastoral ministry can come with energy and from experience. A significant study break of a month or six weeks at around the sixtieth birthday is essential. After that can come a pacing, with regular reviews right up to retirement. We have much to learn about the richness rather than the burn-out of what can be discovered and offered in a significant final time in stipendiary ministry.

- **The practical choices now begin.** Advice needs to be taken about finances and pension benefits. Find out about eligibility for state benefits and the size of the state pension. The Church of England Pensions Board sends an annual statement of the size of the pension on retirement after a full 37 years of service, or eligibility for a proportion of it. The size of the lump sum is also given. From the state, a form called BR19 will tell you the total of your pension and National Insurance contributions and what your total pension will be. At this stage real choices can be explored: to purchase a house with your own money; to sell a private house you may have and trade-up; to take out a shared equity mortgage with the Pensions Board; or to pay rent for one of their houses.

Every diocese runs a pre-retirement course and it is essential that you and your partner begin to attend such courses from your late fifties.

- **The option to take a house for duty post** is open to some. These posts come in almost all dioceses and offer a house free of rent and council tax, maintained by the diocese in exchange for Sunday duty and up to three days' pastoral work per week. This option should not be chosen just because you cannot contemplate ending your clerical lifestyle and pastoral ministry. It is an attractive option for those who were ordained a little later and want a longer run at things. It is available for those who feel that their energy levels are high and who want to work in this way up to their seventieth birthday. It will involve some change of status: most posts of this kind are as assistants to a neighbouring parish where the minister is priest-in-charge of the parish where you will reside and work.

Losses and gains

Retirement will bring an enormous set of changes to you and your partner if you have one. These will also affect your family and your friends. You will lose:

- the public recognition and status of being the vicar in a parish;
- a large house which is maintained and cared for by the diocese;
- a busyness which comes just by being in public life in a parish;
- a whole series of invitations to attend events and social occasions;
- friends and acquaintances which come almost automatically with parish life;
- the payment of many expenses which relate to your work.

You will gain

- freedom to order your day and to do many of the hobbies and activities you dreamed of;
- the security of your church and your state pension;
- the new pleasure of owning your own home and carrying out improvements to it;
- the choice of how much you will continue to do in the rounds of clerical life.

Extra costs

If you have been a stipendiary minister you will have a number of new expenses.

- a mortgage or rent
- house and personal insurance
- council tax and water rates
- the full cost of telephone
- the full cost of heating and lighting your house
- all of the cost of running your car

Priestly ministry in retirement

You will be living in someone else's parish. After what may be thirty or more years of being the vicar, this will seem very strange. It is both a liberation and a constraint. It is liberating because you no longer have the responsibilities of running a parish in what has sometimes felt like a 24-hour on-call job. It is a constraint in that you have to measure your clerical activities and keep a much more low profile since there is another, and younger, person who is the parish priest.

Many clergy say that they want to take a long break, sometimes of up to a year, before they begin to take services again. This allows for a considerable time of refreshment and a total adjustment to retirement freedom away from parochial constraints. Work out how often you will return to your old parish: gradually both you and your former parishioners will establish what is an appropriate level of contact. Depending on your churchmanship, decide whether you will continue with the Daily Offices or your regular prayer and quiet times. Some retired clergy join the parish clergy and often some lay people in saying the Daily Offices in the local parish church. You will also have to work out how often you will be able to receive Holy Communion. The biggest adjustment of all is that you will be sitting in the pews as a member of the congregation!

Public ministry in retirement

Once the retirement event has happened you can decide how much service-taking you will be available to offer. This will need to be negotiated with your new vicar and, more as an offer, with the rural dean. Many parts of the country could not now achieve a full service pattern if it were not for the generous help of the retired clergy. There is a difficult decision about attendance at chapter meetings. Some clergy would not contemplate this at all, others feel it is a supportive place to be. You need to be very sensitive about the appropriateness of too many retired clergy in a chapter, and about the style and level of your contributions.

Sunday duty is a great delight and you will be given a ready welcome in most of the parishes you visit. They will enjoy a new face and voice and be relieved that someone is taking a benevolent interest in them. Take care not to be there every week. It is important for a parish in a vacancy to get a variety of service takers and preachers. You will need to keep yourself updated about changes in the liturgy. It is a great help if a parish in a vacancy can have an annotated service book for visiting celebrants to follow. Do not try to change things or to take a congregation 'back' to the way you used to like to do things!

Sunday duty offers a trap. You will be in many different churches and learn what goes well in a sermon. It is a great temptation to repeat anecdotes and reminiscences over and over again. This will not only bore congregations and your partner but also lead you into staleness. Retirement preaching does not relieve the minister from the discipline of producing new and challenging sermons!

Occasional offices are a different matter from Sunday duty. Especially if your ministry includes funerals, you will still have a pastoral responsibility to visit, delegated from the parish priest. There is now a national agreement that the retired stipendiary priest only keeps two thirds of the fee, with the remainder being paid to the diocese. You will need to keep careful records of your fee income for this purpose as well as for the Inland Revenue.

Spirituality in retirement

One thing is unlikely to change in your retirement: you will still want to say your prayers. But you will have to develop a new discipline. There is no longer the regular pattern of life which parochial ministry has brought. You will not need to be in church at regular times through a week. In some ways you will experience the pressures which lay people feel of finding time to say your prayers. In other ways you will be a priest in retirement and will need to find a pattern of spirituality and prayer which will feed and sustain you in your new lifestyle.

Many clergy may discover a liberating freedom for the first time when they throw off the weight of duty. They may well discover more of the vitality of God in a new openness to worship and a freedom to experience God in the richness of hobbies, travel, relaxation and time with friends and family. The continuation of work with a spiritual director is important. You may also be given an unexpected gain: more people will want to come to you for spiritual guidance when they see that you have some new and really thought-through perspectives to offer.

All of this enriched enjoyment of prayerfulness and spirituality in retirement will have a necessary balance. The Church you served for so long will continue to change. More decisions will be made which change it further. Some of these you will rejoice over, others will make it a Church increasingly different from the one you knew. Liturgy, music, architecture, church furnishings all move on. Sometimes it will seem like a Church you do not understand, one to which you once belonged. All ageing people feel like that, but grace and humility save the situation. Your developing sense of a new spirituality will lead you towards this achievement in ways you will discover with some surprise. They will allow you to accept and embrace the development of a Church searching for new ways of service and liturgical expression in a world which has always changed much more rapidly than the churches set within it.

Part II

Life at the coal-face

IO

Parishes great and small

Things had become pretty slack during the interregnum

Looking for a parish in which to work is a mixture of divine inspiration, advice from friends, the judgement of senior people in the Church, your own intuition and a certain naivety which will allow optimism to triumph over experience. First survey the territory. Deciding on a parish is not like undertaking a battle – or perhaps it is. Military precision suggests that scouts go out and look at the territory, assess the obstacles and weigh the strength and the potential ambushes of the enemy before an advance is planned.

The same but different

To an outsider there are parishes and there are vicars. To an insider there are as many different congregations as there are parishes and as many different vicars as there are trees in the forest. But within the great differences there are types and families of types. I was once in full flight describing the types of people who can be found in congregations in a wonderful conference centre by a beautiful lake in Sweden. Without any reason that I could detect a lady became overcome with tears and had to go out of the room. She was followed by her priest. I thought that it was something I had said, which had perhaps become distorted in translation. It was only at the lunch break, when they came over to apologize, that I discovered the reason. She said that she had been intrigued by my descriptions of the types of people, and their behaviour, which can be found in a congregation. She thought that these people were only in her local church. The thought that there could be similar people causing the same situations all over Europe was too much for her!

When clergy begin to consider which parishes to work in, they need not rely solely on their own experience and intuition. There are clearly some distinct differences of context and size between parishes. Deeply rural or market town communities will be different from those in suburbia or the inner city. Enormous medieval buildings will attract a different type of person from tiny Victorian or ultra modern churches. Clergy and lay people in our much more mobile society will gravitate to the type which suits them. Clergy may want one kind of job when they are setting out and quite another when they have gained experience. Whether a congregation is 'high' or 'low' or has a good musical tradition or is 'touched by renewal' will influence others. Many lay people nowadays choose a congregation because of its openness to newcomers and because it has a recognizable sense of community.

Understanding congregations

Parishes or, more precisely, congregations come in all shapes and sizes. Until fairly recently little work had been carried out on the analysis of parishes and their prevailing characteristics. Information now available is essential reading for any student looking at a first appointment or any clergy considering an appropriate time for a move. Any recommended study and bubble-bursting congregational analysis can be short-circuited by the viewing or reading of the play *Racing Demon* by David Hare. In this he satirizes the life of a team ministry with its intrigues, passions and shades of churchmanship in a way which is too close to truth for comfort. He parodies the often partially-informed personal influence which bishops and others can have on who is, and who is not, appointed to a post. Those looking for a sweeter pill may continue with their reading of Anthony Trollope and the Chronicles of Barchester.

The Alban Institute in the United States has been the pioneer in studying parish life from the 1960s. Its first director, Lauren Mead, with a team of gifted students and writers, has given us a series of studies in congregational size, origins of conflict and very much more. The regular journal and series of publications continue to deepen our understanding of these subjects. In other parts of the world similar institutes have been established. From the early 1970s in Britain, the Edward King Institute for Ministry Development, with its journal, *Ministry*, has tried to hold this ground together with a number of partner organizations.

Others are pursuing parallel courses of study from different traditions in Britain. The Church Growth network has been able to produce better resourced and presented publications to feed a growing evangelical revival in Britain. The Bible Society has reinvented itself, as have the mainstream missionary societies, to engage with questions of mission in a more secularized culture in recent decades.

There should, and should continue to be, a questioning of the appropriateness of parochial structures in a mobile society. Many will argue, with considerable evidence, that people meet in 'village-like' groups for work, hobbies, leisure, in their professions or sets of friendships and it is here that the Church should be found in community. All this having been said and conceded, there is still great evidence that many people find a sense of community in the geographical area in which they live. Those who go to church in the main want to do so close to where they live and they want their children to find modern equivalents of Sunday School there.

Mapping the territory

Ordinands considering their ministry or clergy looking for a change of parish need to have an understanding of the types and sizes of congregation, each with their own characteristics. An understanding of the dynamics of what is happening within these different sized groups is interesting for lay people considering joining, staying in or leaving.

Almost everywhere it is impossible to sustain a pastoral picture of the local clergyperson knowing their people by name and caring in a personal way for all of them. Urban, inner-city ministry has taken on patterns of its own; rural ministry is frequently about 'sharing' one priest or minister between three, four, five or more congregations. Suburban ministry is often about managing congregations of 200 people or more without the support available in Victorian or Edwardian times of several curates, a smattering of layworkers and, according to tradition and denomination, a community of religious sisters. There is no one job description or way of seeing a vicar. Nor is there one way of understanding the life and dynamics of a congregation. Size and situation are important. This is an appropriate point at which to look at an influential piece of analysis done by Roy Oswald of the Alban Institute and to add to it and adapt it for situations other than that of congregations in the United States (see Roy M. Oswald, 'How to minister effectively in family, pastoral, programme and corporate sized churches', Action Information, Alban Institute, March/April 1991).

Family-, Pastoral-, Programme- and Corporate-sized congregations

Basing his analysis on previous work done by Arlin Rothauge, Oswald sets out four basic congregational sizes. Each presents specific sets of behaviour by its members and each requires different methods of working from its ministers. None are absolutely watertight. Some appear to function well even though they are in the wrong category, but life is full of exceptions. I have added a fifth category to take into account the demands made on clergy with more than one parish and on congregations who share one minister. We also need to note, and take into account, the relatively new phenomenon of 'church planting'.

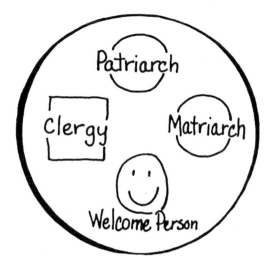

Figure 10.1 A congregation with patriarchs and matriarchs

The small or 'Family'-sized congregation

Small congregations are all too easily seen as problems, ripe for closure or joining with neighbouring parishes, prey to ideas about teams or groups. Clergy can feel undervalued when offered 'charge' of small congregations, which can be regarded, quite wrongly, as places for the sick, for pre-retirement placements or to be shared with an appointment to a specialist ministry post.

What has hardly ever been attempted is an analysis of the life and needs of clergy and people in a small congregation of 40 people or less. Most of us will recognize some distinctive behavioural characteristics from congregations we have known. My wife and I often remark how there are the same people in our various congregations – they just have different names! Roy Oswald calls this a Family-sized church, which has definite and identifiable characteristics.

The Family church with patriarchs and matriarchs

This congregation functions like a family and has appropriate parental figures. These characters defend and control the life of the congregation. They feel a responsibility for its survival and need to preserve and keep traditions which generations of previous patriarchs and matriarchs have thought important.

Defence and survival

Attitudes which are stated as necessary to keep the church open are the very ones which may be contributing to its downfall. So much hard work is being put in by so few that it is difficult for newcomers to get in at all. The key role of the patriarch or matriarch is to see that clergy do not take the surviving congregation off in new directions.

The need for traditional care

These congregations need and expect traditional pastoral care. The minister has to visit all those in the congregation on a regular basis and be available at all times for crises and demands of any kind.

Clergy succeed when they consult

Confrontation will lead to disaster. The only way for a minister to make any progress is to take the needs of the congregation seriously and to listen to what is being said. However difficult, befriending the key people is the only way forward.

Clergy are not taken seriously

Deeply-rooted patriarchal and matriarchal congregations survive by not taking their clergy seriously. 'He or she will only be here for a few years. We can ride their enthusiasms and then go back to what we know when they move on.'

Clergy do not stay

Small congregations are seen as short-stay first appointments or as a last resting place before retirement. Such placement policies by denominations reinforce what these congregations already know – that they are not being taken seriously. Curates are not trained to handle small congregations. They come from 'successful', often suburban, training parishes. They find it hard to work and to stay with the small congregation because their criteria for what works well lie elsewhere.

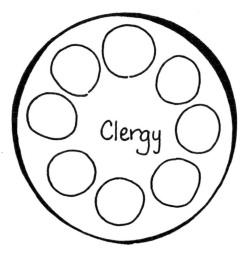

Figure 10.2 The Pastoral congregation

The Pastoral-sized church

Very many people see the congregation with 40 to 130 members as the ideal kind of church. It is the one which is big enough to get things done but small enough for people to know one another by their first names. It is the congregation which will grow most easily by careful attention from the minister who, if they have a mind to, can get around and visit everyone – occasionally! This is the congregation in which training courses can work and where there are just enough people to be able to keep the rotas going. There is enough pledged income to be able to budget and pay the bills. It is the size looked upon favourably by most denominations as 'successful'. However, all concerned are perplexed that this congregation finds it difficult to grow any larger. The benefits of this size of congregation and the demands made upon all concerned go a long way to explain the dilemma.

The minister relates to everyone

Clergy are usually at the centre of a pastoral church. There are so many parental figures around that they want a central person to be the focus for them.

Personal expectations are high

Everyone has an expectation that they will have some kind of personal relationship with the minister. Visiting is expected. Lay people are encouraged to share in the visiting but the real visit is from the vicar. He or she will be expected to be present at every function, or at least to pay a visit.

Growth depends on the minister's popularity

Within a narrow band, compared with the size of the parish, the congregation will add 20–30 people, or lose them, depending on the popularity of the minister. What happens then is up to the skills and resourcefulness of minister and people.

Oppressive demands are felt

As a congregation grows to 100+ the personal demands on the minister become enormous. No one person can cope with the individual expectations of so many people. Delegate or die.

The person at the centre

It is the minister who is the focus of the congregational community. He or she is seen as primarily responsible for recruitment, whether or not this is true. Newcomers can expect to get a personal visit from the minister who is also the principal shepherd of newcomers into the congregation by making invitations and ensuring that they are put on rotas. Present job-holders might move aside if the minister asks.

Hard on the minister's family

The minister's family often say that they feel they are in a sharing agreement with the rest of the congregation. The strains on a marriage are enormous. Great care has to be taken to give time to the family and get time off together.

Size is a block to growth

The greatest problem in congregations of this size is to be able to overcome their minister-focused orientation. Delegation and genuine shared ministries are a must. Lay teams of visitors are essential. Lay leaders need to be identified and trained. A new relationship has to be negotiated with the minister – preferably before heart attack, breakdown or divorce.

The cluster of congregations

Somewhere between the Family and the Pastoral congregation levels, each relating to one minister, is another common situation. This is where several parishes and congregations are brought together with one minister. Much learning needs to be done about these situations. Some interesting pieces of work have been done on rural 'clusters' in follow-up work to the Church of England's report, *Faith in the Countryside*. Details are available from The Arthur Rank Centre, National Agricultural Centre, Stoneleigh Park, Warwickshire CV8 2LZ; www.arthurrankcentre.org.uk. More formally this situation applies to teams and groups, but here more clergy are involved. Several years of work with ministers and people in these clusters has led to the production of this check-list of essentials to be taken into account.

* Always get help with administration. One secretary for all the units can save much frustration. A computer helps enormously with data, lists and in producing the group newsletter.
* Clarify the expectations of the congregations. Do they realize the minister is not theirs exclusively? How much time per week can be given to each congregation?
* Delegate all local responsibilities.
* Agree how expenses will be shared.

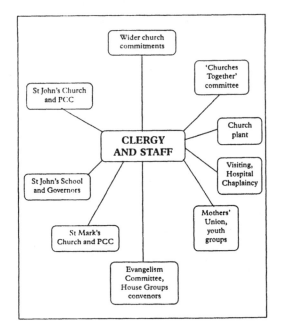

Figure 10.3 The cluster of congregations

* Streamline the pattern of meetings. Avoid duplication wherever possible. Encourage gradual co-operation.
* Establish a regular pattern of services in a month. Services which are at the same time every Sunday help people to get into a routine and remember when to come.
* Decide on a regular day of the week to visit in each community. This also avoids jealousy about where the minister spends time.
* Let everyone know who the local person is for contacts about weddings, baptisms and funeral details.
* Make full use of meeting rooms for local events in each community. Encourage people to travel to support each other's special events.
* Make great use of the fifth Sunday in a month for times of united worship.
* Ensure everyone in each community knows that the vicarage, manse, presbytery is equally theirs. Make it clear how the minister and family want to use it as a public place, if at all.

* It is vital that the minister knows who is related to who in the different communities.
* Get to know the history of co-operation or rivalry between the different communities.
* Understand where the joint meeting places for communities are – schools, Guides and Scouts, Women's Institutes, Rotary, etc. Do not clash or duplicate.

The 'Programme' congregation

Almost too much has been written about the ceiling of 150 or so people which very many congregations with one minister appear to reach. I think that there is a real, and very understandable, sense in which the human-sized congregation or group of people does not want to grow so large that people do not know each other by their Christian names. In a later section I shall suggest that one of the reasons for the appropriateness of church planting is so that congregations can be kept to this human size.

The so-called Programme congregation is one which has managed to break through the numbers ceiling and establish an acceptable new structure. The fundamentally different characteristic of this congregation is that acceptance has been gained for high quality personal contact with the minister to be supplemented by other methods of pastoral care. Lay visitors, support and discussion groups and a devolved, lay-led management structure take the place of the omni-competent minister. A Programme congregation will have many of the following characteristics.

* Several staff members, ordained and lay.
* A well-developed lay leadership who can work well with the staff team. Concepts of 'collaborative ministry' have been explored.
* The principal minister is still central but the role and expectations have been changed. Sometimes a present minister can manage the change as growth takes place. Often illness or strain forces it. A new minister can negotiate and be happier with a different style.
* Good administration takes on a more publicly acknowledged role. The need for systems to assist recruiting, planning, co-ordinating, training and evaluating become obvious.
* One of the principal roles of the minister is to be the pastor to

Figure 10.4 The Programme congregation

the lay leaders and help groups arrive at a consensus around a shared vision.

- 'Unless clergy can learn to derive satisfaction from the work of pastoral administration, they should think twice about accepting the call to such a parish' (Roy Oswald).

The 'Corporate' congregation

Large, famous, eclectic congregations are corporate churches. People attend for a whole range of different reasons from those which attract others to the small, local congregation. Here preaching and the ecclesiastical tradition are important. Such a church may function as a symbol of a particular kind of worship for many others. Congregation members would not expect the principal minister to visit them. Associate ministers and a staff team will have responsibility for all the day-to-day running of the church. Lay leaders and salaried professionals will be responsible for specialized areas of work such as music, pastoral counselling and publishing.

The corporate congregation will have many of these features:

- A high priority will be placed on the quality of the special kind of worship which is being offered.
- Preaching will be very important. Sermons are likely to be recorded and sold.

Figure 10.5 The Corporate congregation

- The musical tradition will be of a very high quality.
- The staff team will spend significant time on sermons and the preparation of worship.
- The senior minister is a symbol of unity and stability.
- The staff team will be collegial but diverse in skills.
- The leadership team will generate energy and momentum for the congregation.
- A very dispersed congregation will be supported by a sophisticated computerized system and a range of new member and renewal programmes.
- The methods of contacting, and following-up, newcomers will be very sophisticated.
- This church is a large-scale financial operation which feeds and supports a range of associated networks doing similar work.

The right size at the right stage

The secret of understanding this analysis of the different size of congregations comes with matching yourself to the appropriate one at the right stage in your ministry. Different personality types of priest also warm to different sizes of congregation.

I have frequently complained of the inappropriateness of training curates in large suburban congregations and then giving them one or two small congregations as a first job. Few of the patriarchal and matriarchal traits experienced in the small congregation are experienced in the suburban one of 100 or more people. There needs to be specific training for work in a small congregation, just as much as for moves from urban to rural situations and vice versa.

Clergy often begin with relatively small congregations and 'graduate' to larger ones. There are many clergy who will find the congregation of 30 or less completely stifling, while others prefer the intimacy of small numbers. There are clergy who want to work with colleagues and others who find this difficult. Some clergy can co-operate with ecumenical colleagues while others find the spread of their own denomination difficult enough!

Knowing what is likely to be going on within the life of a congregation can help in the choice of where to go. It can help even more with understanding the opportunities and tensions within congregations of different size.

Many clergy will move between different size congregations as their ministry develops and as they gain in experience. In one way no two parishes are the same. In another way all parishes have characteristics and similarities. Matching your temperament, the needs of your family and partner to your skills and abilities is a sensitive task. We look next at how moves are made.

The archdeacon says

'Strictly speaking,' said the archdeacon, 'you should have
applied for a faculty'

Legalities in a national Church

Does the Church have its own rules and regulations? How are these
made up? What influence does the state still have on an established

Church? Anyone taking on responsibilities, as a volunteer, paid worker or priest, soon discovers that there is a labyrinth of rules and regulations. Because the Church of England is established, some of its rules are part of the law of England. Other rules come from the Canons and regulations agreed by the Church and its bishops or General Synod. Many other regulations concern the law of the land and apply to every citizen and institution. New clergy and churchwardens find that they face a very steep learning curve when they take up their responsibilities. Every diocese will organize training courses to help and have specialist advisers available at the end of the telephone. The people most able to help and advise are the Registrar, who is the legal officer for the diocese, the Diocesain Secretary and your archdeacon. Every diocese issues a handbook which contains the most important national guidelines and its local regulations. A copy of this will normally be kept in the vestry and another in the possession of the present incumbent or priest-in-charge.

We live in a world constrained by legal requirements and the fear of litigation. One of the biggest changes in recent times for clergy and church councils has been the appearance of a whole range of mandatory legal requirements for running a charitable organization, using public buildings and managing an organization using a whole range of volunteers. Accounts have to be properly kept in a particular way, and records and correspondence have to be stored in a way that provides for appropriate public access. Child protection and child abuse legislation has to be enforced and clergy have to follow published guidelines about their professional conduct when visiting and at other times (see below). Churches and churchyards have to be kept in order and cannot be altered without legal permission.

Parish finances

The Charities Act 1993 makes a whole range of legal demands on a church council, increasing the work of many treasurers and requiring clergy to be even more vigilant about their receipt and use of parish money. All clergy tell horror stories about being given money at a busy moment, stuffing it in a side pocket and only discovering it months later, or forgetting what it was for. Some clergy have been bruised by accusations of receiving money and failing to give it to the treasurer at the earliest opportunity.

It is now essential that clergy account for all money given to them, steer most giving directly to the treasurer and keep a close account of all the fees they earn. Collections from services need to be checked by two people in the church vestry and all Gift Aid envelopes properly, and separately, recorded. Parish treasurers need to carry out their bookkeeping in a standardized way and the person asked to inspect the accounts needs to have some competence.

Many parishes now also have a range of separate financial activities. The largest of these is likely to be a community project of some kind. Hundreds of thousands of pounds come into many of our parishes to employ staff involved in such projects. Even more will come to develop community space in church-owned property. The Church Urban Fund began the concept of community outreach with funded staff for many inner-city parishes. In the years since its creation in 1987 parishes have learned that it is possible to bring in funds from a whole range of sources. The consequences of all this for a parish treasurer is a massive escalation of work, which many treasurers find beyond their ability. More competent people have to be brought in, and often paid, to manage the complex finances of more active parishes. Country churches, unless they are very special, also lend themselves to adaptation for community use and some grants are available here also. When parish finances get to a certain level, a qualified auditor is required to certify the accounts. Fortunately, parish accounts are overseen by the diocese as the major charity to which parish funds relate. Three sets of accounts are sent in with the archdeacon's annual Visitation Questions. One is kept by the archdeacon for personal reference, the other two go to the diocese for scrutiny and are used to help calculate the parish quota or share.

The Data Protection Act 1998

Very little information can be stored nowadays without the named person's permission. Even names, addresses and telephone numbers in the parish magazine should have the person's permission before they are included.

Clergy and parish officers storing information electronically or in paper-based files should be aware that this information can be requested by those concerned. It is now very important that sensitive material is stored in the right way, and it often requires the person's permission. One consequence of this sensitivity is that much more information and the content of many files are destroyed to avoid the risk of unfortunate information becoming available to the public or those concerned.

If information about individuals is stored electronically, the Data Protection Act requires that the person responsible for that file be registered. The Information Commissioner keeps a public register of all data controllers. Registration can be done through the designated officer in each diocese or by making direct contact with the Office of the Information Commissioner, through their website, www.dpr.gov.uk, by letter to Wycliffe House, Water Lane, Wilmslow, Cheshire SK9 5AF, or by telephoning the Information helpline 01625 545745 or the Notification Helpline 01625 545740.

Guidelines for pastoral care

The days have long gone when male clergy could visit ladies alone in their own homes. The old pastoral manner of most clergy, touching the person they are visiting, holding their hand or arm, even giving a 'hug', is no longer appropriate. Every diocese, and now the House of Bishops, has issued guidelines for good pastoral practice among clergy. This is not a document to be filed and left unread. Accusations, whether founded or not, are made with great frequency and there is usually no-one to verify or deny an accusation. Only the minister and the person making the complaint are present and it is one person's word against another. A careful reading of the guidelines will at least help clergy to avoid getting themselves into situations where misunderstandings can occur.

All clergy and ministers are called to represent Christ in their dealings with other people. A number of guidelines include a check-list to help clergy behave in professionally appropriate ways when visiting or working with other people; this check-list will include the following points.

Ministers should:

- behave at all times in a way that will honour God and communicate the gospel, and maintain a high standard of professionalism in all aspects of ministry;
- help to develop an environment of trust and love within the

community of the Church, and work to establish and maintain good relationships with those in the wider community;

- act in a way that shows that the Church is concerned with the pastoral care and wellbeing of others;
- seek to keep a balance between parochial and personal/family responsibilities;
- act in a way that justifies and maintains public trust and confidence in ministers of the Church;
- seek the very best for parishioners and others in their pastoral care, and any who they supervise, encouraging all people to grow and develop rather than become increasingly dependent on the minister or others;
- be aware of the power they hold in any pastoral relationship and the consequent vulnerability of any parishioner;
- pay attention, in any pastoral interview, to the appropriateness of the setting, time of day, body language, touch and terms of endearment, and if there are regular meetings with young people, be aware of the need to have someone else present;
- take responsibility for their own on-going training and personal development;
- if they are in regular contact with vulnerable people, undertake supervision themselves so that the highest professional standards can be maintained;
- decline any duties or responsibilities which are beyond their competence, and seek specialist advice when necessary;
- ensure that lay or ordained ministers within their oversight are aware of the standards applicable in all Christian ministry, and that they possess the skills and knowledge to be able to discharge their roles competently;
- maintain a high standard of confidentiality, protect all confidential information about parishioners, and make disclosures on them only when justified, and usually with the person's consent;
- involve themselves in appropriate forms of appraisal;
- expect to be accountable for advice given and decisions made.

Ministers should not:

- undertake any professional duties while under the influence of alcohol or drugs;

- abuse the privileged relationship between minister and parishioner, the privileged access this gives them to a person, home, property or workplace, or the privileged relationship between themselves and colleagues or trainees;
- discriminate against anyone on the grounds of race, ethnic origin, religious belief, gender, sexuality, age, disability, or any other matter that would cause anyone to be treated with injustice;
- deal with church finances in such a way that personal and church monies become confused;
- enter into any pastoral relationship in order to receive any personal advantage or gain, whether monetary, emotional, sexual or material;
- seek to represent a personal opinion or viewpoint for which they are not trained or which they are not competent to provide;
- enter into a 'counselling' relationship for which they are not qualified;
- say, 'It will never happen to me!'

Child protection and child abuse

In 1995 the House of Bishops issued a Policy Statement on Child Abuse and recommended its implementation in every diocese. Essentially, this means that the Church of England accepts the intention of the Children Act 1989 that the interests and welfare of children is paramount in any community. The Act defines a child as a person under the age of 18 years.

Each diocese has now appointed an Adviser in Child Protection and Child Abuse Issues. One of their jobs is to ensure that every parish is aware that it has a direct responsibility for ensuring the protection of children while they are in the care of its officers or volunteers. Each PCC has to appoint one or more of its members to act as their representative to oversee the implementation of the policy within the life and work of the congregation. They will keep a register of all those who, on behalf of the minister and PCC, are responsible for work with those under the age of 18. All those who undertake this work, including the minister, should have appropriate references taken up and have been 'cleared for work' by having their details checked through the Criminal Records Bureau.

Sex offenders and the congregation

A congregation may include a person who has been convicted of a sex offence. This is defined as rape, indecent assault, gross indecency, incest, related offences to do with pornographic material, or indecent exposure. This whole subject area is highly emotive, but needs to be regarded with the utmost seriousness by every congregation and minister. It is an area where rumour and innuendo should be quickly contained but where every accusation needs to be taken seriously.

When an allegation has been made, the priest responsible for that congregation should contact the Diocesan Child Protection Officer, who will be able to offer reassurance as well as make confidential checks about the accused person. It is also appropriate to bring in the parish's Child Protection Representative at this stage, and I have always found it good practice to confide in my churchwardens whenever possible. This whole subject is not easy for priests or for congregations. Congregations are most susceptible to rumour. Clergy often feel that their pastoral skills can help; many of them have now undertaken some basic training in this area and are on their guard against the manipulation which is characteristic of such offenders. Equally, many clergy will want to believe that repentance, a change of heart and forgiveness are possible, but in this particular area it is better to be cautious. The truly repentant will be willing to keep all restrictions placed on them. Any element of wanting to negotiate on this should set off warning bells to those who have received a basic training.

Official guidance and publications

In *Meeting the Challenge: how the churches should respond to sex offenders* (Church House Publishing, 1999), there is an information sheet which gives clear guidelines about how known offenders might be integrated into a congregation.

- Where a known offender joins a church it will be important to extend love and friendship to the individual and their families, but at the same time the leadership will need to ensure that a frank discussion takes place with the person concerned and that efforts are made to sustain open communication.

- It will be necessary to establish clear boundaries for both the protection of the young people and to lessen the possibility of the adult being wrongfully accused of abuse.

The following points should be addressed:

- Church leaders should ensure they maintain close links with the Probation Service.
- Be open with the offender.
- Prepare a contract which includes:
    - attending designated meetings only
    - sitting apart from children
    - staying away from parts of the building where children meet
    - attending a house group where there are no children
    - declining hospitality where there are children
    - never being alone with children
    - never working with children.
- Get the offender to sign a contract.
- Enforce the contract – manipulation is a characteristic of many offenders.
- Consider how much to tell the PCC and wider congregation.
- Ensure that churchwardens and key leaders know the situation.
- Provide close support and pastoral care.
- Ban the offender from church if the contract is broken. Tell other churches and the Probation Service.

The care of church buildings

Hardly anything can be moved in a church without permission. Few things can be brought in and no significant repairs can be done without some other authority being contacted. Clergy and churchwardens in law own the church building, the churchyard and the church furnishings. To allow changes to take place, the Church of England is in a privileged position. It has ecclesiastical exemption from most areas of planning permission, though local authorities still have to be consulted about many changes to buildings.

The system which operates in the Church of England is administered by the Chancellor of the diocese, who grants faculties for work to be done, the archdeacon, who also grants faculties and gives de minimis letters for minor changes, and the Diocesan Advisory Committee, which considers all applications for faculties.

There is a simple rule-of-thumb way to determine when permission is required to do anything in a church building. If the answer to the question, 'Will it look different if you do this?' is 'yes', then permission of some kind is needed. The best advice is to ask first and consult with relevant bodies at an early stage.

The archdeacon and members of a Diocesan Advisory Committee will visit a church on request to discuss any plans at an early stage. They can advise on layout, positioning of furnishings, the use of materials and colour and much more. If this is done before a request for a faculty is petitioned, the path will be much easier.

Applications for a faculty which are not contentious are granted by the archdeacon. Anything else needs to take a longer route. If a building is of any kind of architectural interest, then the appropriate amenity society needs to be contacted. If the floor or churchyard is to be dug up, archaeological advice needs to be sought. If trees are involved, an arboriculturalist needs to be consulted. The same type of consultation is needed for glass, bells, organs and clocks.

If there is general agreement among the PCC and a recommendation from the DAC, then a petition for a faculty can go to the Chancellor. After examining the case, the proposals are made public by notices being placed in the church porch for 28 days. If there are no objectors then a faculty can be granted. If there are significant objections, from members of the congregation, the public, or the amenity societies, the Chancellor of the diocese will hold a consistory court and make a judgement.

No work of any significant kind can be done without a faculty. If work is carried out prematurely, an order can be given for it to be reversed. On occasions a confirmatory faculty can be given after work is done, but the PCC will probably have to pay the full costs of this. Most dioceses pay for faculties which are granted after due consultation from their Share or Quota income.

Responsibility for the care of church buildings

Responsibility for the regular care of church buildings rests with the incumbent, the churchwardens and the PCC. Each church building must be inspected by an approved architect every five years. This inspection comes to the PCC, the archdeacon and the DAC in a standardized form as a Quinquennial Report. It will have a detailed description of the condition of the interior, exterior, roof and many fixtures of the building. At the back will be a summary of works needed to be carried out immediately, those which should be done within one year and those which can be phased over five years. These reports are not a specification and professional people need to become involved before any work is begun.

PCCs need to budget for and spend often significant sums of money each year to keep their building in order. If they do not, then major expenditure will accumulate. If a building is listed as Grade 1 or as Grade 2* then it is possible that English Heritage will provide some funding. Larger sums may be available from the Joint Grant Scheme administered by the Community Fund (formerly the National Lottery Charities Board) and English Heritage. Not all PCCs are happy to apply for lottery money; this has to be a local decision.

The archdeacon is required by law to inspect each church building in the archdeaconry once every three years, using the Quinquennial Report. Such a visit will now include a tour of the churchyard to check gravestones for safety and examine boundary walls, and nowadays the archdeacon will also ask to inspect the parish's child protection files. The care of records and registers will be examined on the same visit.

Records and registers

All ancient churches will have records which date back more than 100 years. These need to be stored in dry conditions which are also fireproof and at an approved level of humidity, and the church has to purchase an appropriate container or, preferably, deposit its records and registers in the County Record Office.

Every diocese has a Records and Registers Officer, who is often a trained archivist or historian. They will come and look through parish records, registers and papers, catalogue them for the PCC and advise on the best place for them to be kept. It is now normal practice for them to visit a parish church at the time of a vacancy to inspect the records. The archdeacon will make a legal inspection at the time of the three-yearly parish visitation.

Deposited papers and registers remain in the ownership of the PCC and many Record Offices will make microfiche copies available for the PCC. Requests for copies of entries in registers can be made to a PCC. They will decide and give permission according to the applicant.

Always ask

There is only one piece of sound advice which needs to be given with regard to the contents of this chapter: *ask for advice before you say or do anything* – certainly before you meet objecting groups or individuals, and definitely before you write anything down! Every diocese has a series of officers whose responsibility it is to give advice. They are available at a telephone call or with a letter to the Diocesan Office.

The archdeacon is always available and has gained general and legal experience which will both reassure and direct. The Secretary of the Diocesan Advisory Committee will advise on church buildings matters, the Registrar on all legal matters. The Diocesan Child Protection Officer is always available with support and the necessary detailed information. The Records and Registers Officer will arrange a visit to look at any papers which are of concern. Pastoral matters should be referred to the rural dean, the archdeacon or, depending on their nature and seriousness, to the suffragan or area bishop or the diocesan bishop through his chaplain or PA.

Clergy and PCCs can either feel exposed in difficult situations or tangled up in red tape and ancient legal history. Advice, usually freely given, is the best route to take. If you do not know, it is impossible to guess with church regulations; you need to ask. The penalties for not asking are often difficult public confrontations, an awkward press and a nasty atmosphere in the parish and community. Sound, wise advice can help the local clergy to make the right decisions. If officers of the diocese have been consulted first it is easier for them to support clergy who find themselves in sensitive local situations.

12

Managing the vicarage tea party

Brian was always open to constructive criticism

There are some times when work in the Church of England feels like living on George Orwell's *Animal Farm*. The pigs have taken over and the workhorses do all the work! Then I think about when I used to cycle around London. As a cyclist the cars and the pedestrians were the enemy. When I drive a car around London the cyclists are always in the way. When I walk around London I condemn the cars and curse the cyclists! It all depends on your perspective. So it is with attitudes to management and leadership within any organization. However, for the churches there are strong guidelines from the Bible about leadership, a Christ-like ministry and order within the Church. These have to be developed alongside acceptable attitudes to leadership within any generation. The challenge today seems to be to develop a leadership within our churches which reflects the needs of today and does not rely on methods of leadership from any previous generation.

Parables and analogies

With what shall we compare leadership and management within the churches? There is the example of *Animal Farm*, which was thought to be a satire on the Soviet system of government. In the life of the Church of England it might be a helpful discussion starter to look at the role of bishops and their relationship to the clergy. There are, however, stronger and less historically determined examples. These all begin with the ministry of Jesus and his strong words about the leader needing to be the servant of all. There are times when a leader has to take or accept leadership initiatives. Here examples from David or Saul or Solomon come into play. At other times leaders have to be prophetic and then there is a great biblical tradition which can be visited.

There are shelves of tomes about management in all large bookshops. Many of them will be helpful for clergy working out their role and tasks in a parish. There is also much anecdotal wisdom. Much folklore about wise practice in leading and managing is gathered from parables and proverbs.

Management versus leadership

It is necessary at this point to draw a distinction between managing and leading. I rather like this saying to distinguish leadership from management: 'Management is doing things right. Leadership is doing the right things. Management is efficiency in climbing the ladder of success; leadership determines whether the ladder is leaning against the right wall.' Managing is about maintaining what is there and making sure everything works to its maximum efficiency. When things begin to go awry it is good management which can return an organization to stability. It has been said, however, that even good management is 'the maintenance and achievement of pre-defined goals, most of which are set or inspired by leaders'. Consequently, leadership is something which happens on the edge, at the boundaries, of organizations. It challenges accepted conventions, it debates and encourages the emergence of new visions and green shoots. It can pick up a failing organization and rejuvenate it by focusing the willing around a renewed vision. Leading has a distinct personality aspect. That is why an element of humility is necessary in the personal qualities of leaders. At the same time an absolute belief is often needed in the concept or idea which is the subject of leadership. Leadership is a visionary, prophetic and enabling activity, inside or outside the Church. It challenges the given, offers alternatives and inspires those who catch the vision to enable alternatives to become realities. Visions become realities which are deliverable when leaders have good managers who want to work with them.

A negative reaction

There has been a generation or more in English churches which has reacted in a very negative way to concepts of management in the Church. Others, often among the leadership, have followed secular fashion in trying to bring organizational ideas into the Church. We are now at a time when tremendous questions face bishops and parish clergy alike about how they are to enable the organization to adapt, change and develop. Keeping the system going is placing an enormous strain on all those involved. The far fewer numbers of stipendiary clergy and the great increase in the cost of financing the Church means that significant change, and a more focused concentration on key tasks, is inevitable. It will need important leadership styles to be named and explored. Negativity may be the reaction to some bad experiences of employment in the secular world. For others it may be a means of avoidance when serious issues need to be faced.

Job descriptions

The Prayer Books which we have give key job descriptions for bishops, priests and deacons.

Diaconal work is primarily a ministry of service. There is a strong movement across Europe to promote the concept of a permanent diaconate and to re-establish this Office within the Church. 'A deacon is called to serve the Church of God, and to work with all its members in caring for the poor, the needy, the sick, and all who are in trouble.'

Priests are also deacons throughout their ministry and the element of service is always there. Additionally there is a specific place within the Church for priestly ministry.

> A priest is called by God to . . . proclaim the word of the Lord, to call hearers to repentance, and in Christ's name to absolve, and to declare the forgiveness of sins. He or She is called to baptise, and to prepare the baptised for confirmation, to preside at the celebration of the Holy Communion, to lead people in prayer and worship, to intercede for them, to bless them in the name of the Lord and to teach and encourage by word and example. He or She is to minister to the sick, and prepare the dying for their death. They must set the Good Shepherd before them as the pattern of their calling by caring for the people committed to their charge and joining with them in a common witness to the world.

Bishops also have a job description in the charge of their consecration service:

> A bishop is called to lead in serving and caring for the people of God and to work with them in the oversight of the Church. As chief pastor he shares with his fellow bishops a special responsibility to maintain and further the unity of the Church, to uphold its discipline and to guard its faith. . . . He is to be merciful, but with firmness, and to minister discipline, but with mercy. He is to have a special care for the outcast and the needy; and to those who turn to God he is to declare the forgiveness of sins.

In diocesan manuals there are job descriptions for rural and area deans. There has to be a job description for a new archdeacon as part of the appointment process. An exploration of how these descriptions are interpreted and applied has to follow.

Teaching leadership and management

One major area which is not covered in any systematic way by colleges or courses before ordination, or in post-ordination training or inservice training, is how to lead and how to manage. There are short courses in pastoral skills and counselling within most schemes and in the programmes of most dioceses. There is hardly anything about management and leadership. The situation is becoming particularly strange now that it is clear that many clergy will be either looking after very large parishes, some with significant funding in community projects, or having the care of a whole grouping of smaller parishes. While there are fewer curates, there are more paid lay staff. An increasing number of clergy are being encouraged to work in groups and teams.

Those who are trying to encourage the study and teaching of leadership within the denominations are all in small voluntary groupings on the edge of the churches. The organization called MODEM (Managerial and Organizational Disciplines for the Enhancement of Ministry), of which I am a part, has been set up to encourage the exchange of good practice between church organizations and those in the voluntary and private sectors. The Leadership Institute based in Cambridge provides extended courses in analysis and reflection on work for clergy and church leaders. The Edward King Institute for Ministry Development encourages the exchange of good practice within the parochial and local ministry spheres. The Grubb Institute has offered courses and produced publications on organizational analysis for a number of years. A list of key course and resource providers can be found in the 'Bibliography and resources' section at the end of this book.

Why the need for management?

'Responsible stewardship' is all that is needed to answer this question. If there is a crisis in vocations, in the commitment of members to attend church frequently, or in the availability of money to fund the Church, it all comes down to a belief in the responsible stewardship of the resources which the churches have. However strong the calling to priesthood, if the tasks required are approaching the impossible in their demands, then the response cannot be effective. Unless parishes and dioceses, and the Church Commissioners, demonstrate time and time again that they are making the best possible use of money given or held in trust, then funding the work will always be a struggle. If the management of the way in which the faith is presented is not clear, then levels of commitment will be low. All of this asks not that churches hire business schools and management consultants to reorganize them, but that churches draw from their resources key concepts which will determine the style of ministry required, yearned for, in order to reconstruct a viable Church for the future.

What is 'good' leadership?

Denominations have different cultures and quite different beliefs about their internal structures. Episcopally-led churches have a built-in hierarchical and synodical structure. Reformed churches will have a significant bias towards the involvement or governance of their denomination by members. The Revd Dr Bill Allen has researched leadership from a Baptist Church perspective. In the April 2002 edition of the MODEM newsletter he says that three of the six Baptist theological colleges are moving towards the inclusion of leadership development within the curriculum of their vocational courses. His research in Baptist congregations has identified what members value in the leadership of 'good' ministers. He has identified six 'core qualities and skills':

- Spirituality
- Interpersonal skills
- Personal qualities
- Management
- Communication skills
- Leadership.

Dr Allen says that the character and qualities of a minister were found to be as significant as the skills required for the office and role of a minister. This has led to the construction of three fundamental questions for initial and inservice training:

- What should the Christian minister know? (knowledge)
- What should the Christian minister be? (character)
- What should the Christian minister do? (skills)

This has led to a diagram which can inform the structure of ministerial review:

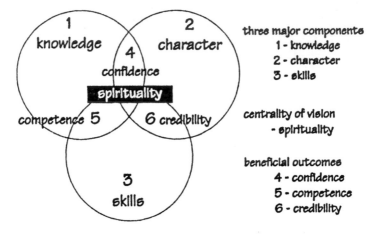

Figure 12.1 Core qualities and skills

People qualities in management

The churches have been helped over many years to understand their internal workings by Professor Gillian Stamp, who works from Brunel University. From her early work with deaneries she has made herself available to church leaders for consultations and conferences on a wide range of subjects in the area of leadership. For me, one of her most memorable articles is 'Stealing the Churches' Clothes'. In this she tells how, in her secular research and work, she hears companies using language and concepts about relating to people which she would more probably expect to hear from the churches, but does not. Writing in the April 2002 MODEM newsletter she distils four key qualities which church leadership might bring as an offering to the wider world.

Discernment

For centuries the word 'discernment' was used in relation to objective spiritual guidance. Gillian Stamp says that it is now used to describe the art of picking up on the 'regular irregularities' which thread through turbulent situations and which can be used to ease things forward. In a culture where it is now acceptable for faith leaders to make a major contribution to public life, this key skill needs further refinement and can be made as a significant offering to the wider life of communities.

Understanding

A second skill which is much sought-after in secular organizations is the way in which people can be supported as they seek meaning in what they do. 'Believing in' one's work and being able to offer it to God has been a key theme in the consultations in which I and my colleagues have attempted to connect faith with people's work. Understanding why, and for what purpose, work is being done contributes to a sense of worth and purpose in the person carrying out the tasks.

Forgiveness

A third skill which Gillian Stamp believes Christians can offer is around the concept of forgiveness – the capacity to move beyond blame to learning. The word 'forgiveness' can feel awkward and may be a concept not easily understood by secular organizations. When embraced, possibly dressed in different language, it can enable a liberation from an unhealthy focusing on the offence or problem and a movement towards review, learning, reconciliation and a new direction.

Reflection

The encouragement of reflection increases self-awareness. Gillian Stamp suggests that the resources which churches have might be offered in the training of leaders. Her article ends with a significant quotation from the Quaker scholar Parker J. Palmer:

A leader is a person who has an unusual degree of power to project on other people his or her shadow, his or her light. A leader is a person who has an unusual degree of power to create the condition under which other people must live and move and have their being . . . a leader is a person who must take special responsibility for what is going on inside him or herself . . . lest the act of leadership create more harm than good.

The Bible has many examples of how power can be used and abused, and of how it was transformed in the way Jesus interpreted his life.

Transitional leadership

There is no last word on leadership or management. We are all aware that 'cannot manage a vicarage tea party' is used as a term of derision for those who are thought to be incompetent. No chapter or book can be an adequate response to such a caricature, even if one were appropriate. For my conclusion I want to develop words and concepts which appear to be based in faith and spirituality and now seem to be emerging as one 'model' of leadership evolves into another.

Strategist to Visionary

Long-term plans and structural reorganizations have wearied people and not delivered very much. There has been a traditional model of leadership which has relied on the development of strategies in order to achieve stated goals. Management by objectives has been a well-used concept. People are not enlivened by strategies. There is a sense that people in organizations and churches want to understand *why* they should do something rather than simply *what* they should do. It is often said that Martin Luther King's 'I have a dream' speech was a vision statement: people believed because he believed. Leaders in the future will embody a vision in themselves, by who they are and by how they communicate what they believe. Strategy has a sense of the dead hand about it; vision fires the imagination and paints a picture in the mind of how things can be.

Commander to Storyteller

Command and control has been an effective model for many who are committed to hierarchical leadership. People, including the laity in the churches, vote with their feet and are not willing to be told what to do. There is a strong sense that many more people are looking for meaning in what they do – to believe in their occupation – rather than to receive orders. We all respond better to encouragement and example than to dictat.

Hugh Burgess, in a paper about leadership in the churches for a meeting sharing Anglican-Lutheran conversations after the Porvoo Agreement, says:

Effective leaders no longer command, they tell stories – and I don't mean lies – but they show one group of people how another has faced, tackled and overcome particular difficulties. They demonstrate by example. I suppose it is, in part, helping to create the vision but it's also the practical working out of that vision into action. The leader doesn't do it – the people do it but by being shown the possibilities and doing it themselves.

Engineers into Servants

Traditionally, leaders have constructed organizations to achieve tasks and in so doing have defined the processes to be used. In an age of rapid change, where organizations are continually being re-engineered, this is no longer practical. The approach is increasingly to enable people to make decisions for themselves. It is becoming true that many new-style leaders do not demand change, even by their inspirational example; they demand that others challenge the status quo. Leaders are increasingly focusing on developing initiatives in others and supporting their ideas. This 'developmental' approach is central to most community work and is an essential concept for church leaders as they exercise the kind of oversight which will enable the whole People of God to participate in the re-shaping of the churches.

The end is the beginning

Jesus returned those who questioned him to themselves and what was at the heart of their questioning. Good leaders and effective managers listen to their people. They listen also to those who come with questions from outside. Leaders gain a response through who they have shaped themselves to become. They lead by a vision which inspires themselves and others. Our Christian leaders draw their inspiration from the source of their faith. Good managers of any kind can see ways in which things might be done. The manager enabling people to achieve and be creative is playing a key part in what Christians would call the unfolding of the Kingdom of God here in earth. All of our belief is about a vision for the future –

our faith is in the possibilities of God's Kingdom being unfolded in this world order. Part of that work is entrusted to those who lead and those who manage.

All together now

For a while, the argument seemed to favour
'The English Hymnal'

Collaborative ministry

Collaborative ministry is certainly central to the thinking of all
those who want to see a revitalization of congregational life. I have
already described how the ability to work collaboratively is one of
the criteria used in the selection process for clergy. Changes in the

number of clergy available to work in parishes mean that they often have to work with one or more congregations. Group and team ministries involve complex patterns of work between clergy and groups of lay people in different parishes. Congregations can suffer if clergy are seen to block new ideas. Consequently the current climate sees collaborative patterns of ministry as a good thing. We are also in a church where no-one quite knows what these words mean and there is little written material available to help. Experiment is stimulating but does result in some nasty bruises and can hurt people. We all learn in part through getting things right in spite of making mistakes.

The Church of England report, *Working as One Body*, attempts a small look at how we can work collaboratively in a church which is essentially hierarchical. Looking at its own structures, the report says that while episcopacy is one of its core structures, the Church has developed a way of governing through a managed interaction of its different parts – episcopal, synodical and legal.

> 'Episcope' (literally 'oversight') involves preserving a synoptic vision of the whole, together with responsibilities for ensuring the co-ordination of each aspect of the mission of the Church. . . . To be the people of God means to live in a certain quality of personal, face-to-face relationships, embodying God's reconciliation of all things in Christ, living in the light of God's justice, forgiveness and new life. (p. 5)

A Roman Catholic view

The Roman Catholic Bishops' Conference of England and Wales has also produced a report on collaborative ministry called *The Sign We Give*, in which they try to wrestle with the relatively new concepts of a clergy and laity deliberately working together in diocesan and congregational life. Coming from a more overtly hierarchical background, this is a publication inspired by a freshness of approach.

It begins with a reflection on Vatican II, where the foundation of collaborative ministry was laid and emphasis was given to the place of lay people in the life of the Church. While agreeing that collaborative ministry is hard to define, they begin with the concept of communion:

the ability to co-ordinate all the gifts and charisms of the
community, to discern them and put them to good use for
the upbuilding of the Church in constant union with the
Bishops. . . . Collaborative ministry is not only the focus for
growth or renewal in the Church today. Rather, it is one way
of expressing how the church renews itself. (p. 13, quoted from
Pope John Paul II, 'Pastores dabo vobis', 1992)

The report concedes that some parishes have learned their lessons
by going directly for a collaborative approach, while others have
begun by working with particular community groups or listening
to those with special concerns such as women in the Church. In
all this there is an important overlap between priestly formation,
inservice training, and the movement from an authoritative to a
collaborative model of working.

In the section 'Collaborative Ministry: Experience and theology'
(p. 17) there are some helpful attempts at the necessary ingredients
for a definition:

• Collaborative ministry is a way of relating and working together
  which expresses the communion which the Church is given and
  to which it is called.
• Collaborative ministry brings together into partnership people
  who, through baptism and confirmation, as well as ordination
  and marriage, have different vocations, gifts and offices within
  the Church.
• Involvement in collaborative ministry demands conscious commitment to certain values and convictions.
• Collaborative ministry begins from a fundamental desire to work
  together because we are called by the Lord to be a company of
  disciples, not isolated individuals.
• Collaborative ministry is committed to mission. It is not simply
  concerned with the internal life of the Church. Rather it shows
  to the world the possibility of transformation, of community and
  of unity within diversity.

There is then developed a theology of collaborative ministry
through the concepts of service based on baptism and confirmation,
to which all are called and which are reflected in worship and in
action. 'Those who do participate actively begin to discover this

theology by doing so. For many others, it continues to remain a closed book'! There is an instructive two-way dialogue which is always taking place between church and world.

The question of authority is faced in two ways: the authority of all the baptized, and the authority of orders or office within the Church. As collaborative ministry gets into the bloodstream of a congregation there will emerge new images of leadership. The authors of the report were attracted to the idea of the leader as 'moderator of the aspirations, plans and priorities of a community, always holding the common good before them.' The primary task of the priest is to enable communion to grow, rather than 'to run the parish'. There are important concepts here for all denominations.

The 'nots' of collaborative ministry are also outlined:
– not strong lay involvement but little collaboration;
– not just lay people having parts in the liturgy;
– not changed structures without consultation in decision-
   making.

Spread throughout the rest of the report are pointers to the essentials of good practice:

- Collaborative ministry does not happen just because people work together or co-operate in some way. It is a gradual and mutual evolution of new patterns.
- Collaborative ministry is built upon good personal relationships.
- Collaborative teams, where personal relationships are important, highlight the importance of emotional maturity.
- Collaborative parishes and teams generally place a high priority on developing a shared vision, often expressed in a mission statement, or in regularly reviewed aims and objectives.
- The courage to face and work through conflict, negotiating until a compromise is found, and even seeking help in order to resolve it, are not weaknesses but signs of maturity and commitment.
- The desire for shared decision-making is the natural outcome of working collaboratively.
- Some decisions, especially those that set policy or touch on matters of critical importance to the community, can be shared widely and arrived at by consensus.

- Fear among priests and lay people that collaborative ministry will leave them little to do is a major barrier.
- Lack of continuity in ministerial appointments can frustrate collaborative ministry.
- Those working in collaborative teams have to recognize personal and professional boundaries and reconcile these with differing individual situations.
- It is increasingly recognized that men and women characteristically have different ways of communicating and can easily misunderstand each other's needs and intentions.
- Teams need to work very hard at how they communicate, and enable different members to take responsibility for what they think and feel.

Collaborative leadership in mission

Two Boards of the Church of England have a working group which is exploring examples of good practice in local collaborative ministry. It is also looking at the intriguing concept of where elements of leadership and mission come into this method of working.

The working group's task has begun with a look at how groups and teams, or local collaborative clusters, have come into existence. The impetus has been very much a mixture of an enterprising individual, a group of people who want to work together in order to get something done, and a group of people who are willing to be open and honest about their feelings of working with one another.

A series of stages have been identified in the development of a learning process which enables collaborative work to progress:

1. A first-level effectiveness group or team has dealt with its process – i.e. the members have been willing to examine who they are and how they work together.
2. A group or team is created and developed with functioning capabilities – one which is capable of getting things done.
3. This co-operative exercise leads to, or unconsciously becomes, a high performing team with evident significant reflective and review capabilities. It realizes that it does not know enough to move on to complete tasks or begin new ones.
4. It knows that it does not know enough, but *how* does it know that it does not know enough?

5. The question of 'how to know' is resolved by the team choosing to develop each other as well as the work. As people get to know one another in greater depth a high level of trust is developed and people become more secure in themselves.
6. If the members of a team/work group are changed by this process, and by the work achieved, then they have to start again, *but . . .*
7. Through the experience of the work they have been trained as a team players.

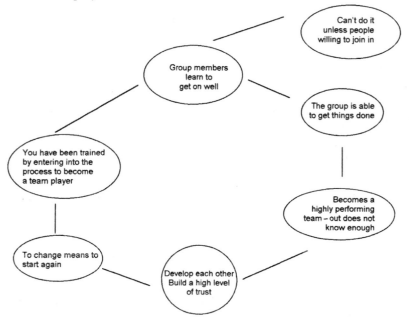

Figure 13.1 The cycle of development for collaborative working

Collaborative abuse by clergy

Some of the most over-used words of today are about 'shared ministry'. I have seen them so abused that clergy, especially those who have strong hierarchical preferences, go completely overboard and abdicate all responsibility and all leadership. One congregation described it to me as 'Over to you, I am off to the golf course.' I have seen others abuse shared ministry so that it becomes just another way of jobs being shared out, but with the minister retaining control.

Collaborative congregational development

What is required in our exploration of collaborative ministry is an understanding of the nature of church life as reflected in a changing relationship between minister and people. I want to achieve this by looking at a series of ways in which clergy can choose to work with their people. These ideas were first developed by myself and my colleague at Avec, Revd Dr Henry Grant, SJ, who began this thinking with Base Communities in Paraguay (Avec is a training and consultancy agency begun by Dr George Lovell and Catherine Widdicombe in 1976 and now carried on by trained volunteers and the founders in retirement; I was Director, 1991–4). We were able to develop it with a number of pieces of parish work in Britain and Ireland.

Figure 13.2 A minister-dominated congregation

A minister-dominated congregation

A hierarchically structured congregation looks the same in any denomination. The minister does almost everything. That is why they are ministers, it is why they studied and were ordained. The minister 'ministers to' the people. The people want to be ministered to. They are a type of 'clients' to the minister. The attitude of letting themselves be served predominates.

The minister tries to satisfy everyone's wishes. This preoccupation with wanting to please everyone causes many sleepless nights. Each group in the congregation makes its own demands – the minister should visit all the families, should take communion to the sick and should spend time with each old person. The minister has to offer interesting trips for young people, try to reconcile fighting married couples, prepare interesting services, edit the parish

Figure 13.3 The compliant congregation with
some participation

newsletter, raise money to repair the church, for the central funds and to give away. And if the minister dies of a heart attack or leaves, it is hoped that the next person will do all that and even more!

Here is the beginning of shared ministry. People begin to share in the work of carrying out the many tasks which need to be done in a parish. There are lively debates in the church council. People are encouraged to form groups to organize tasks and house groups take place around specific themes. The servers' group meets without the minister, as do the choir and mothers' group. The Alpha or Emmaus groups or Catechumenate welcome newcomers.

Shared ministry is beginning and the congregation is developing more responsibility for its own life. But where is the minister? Has the role ever been discussed? Is this some new conversion? Have they been away on a course? Unless the change of role for the minister is understood they can appear to be absent from the changes, marginalized, the cause of a vacuum in a key place.

Gradually in the discussion groups, the confirmation preparation and informally at the social gatherings, congregation members

Figure 13.4 A congregation which begins to think

begin to ask one another what is going on. They begin to enjoy their new responsibilities, but more than that they see what they are doing in terms of their Christian discipleship. They are not just experiencing more busyness and activity as the minister relinquishes hold of all activities; they begin to see what they are doing as having some connection with the faith they are understanding anew through these discussions and through their new responsibilities. Questions like, 'What is going on in this congregation?' begin to spring up. Even more hopefully, people begin to ask questions about the congregation from the other end. 'What is it for? What are we here for? What is the church for?' In their debates thinking begins about what it means to be an adult believer today, and what kind of church is needed to support such adult belief, spiritual development and Christian service.

A collective and idealized way of expressing these new experiences might be the following: 'As a lay person I am not just a helper in the tasks which the minister has done before; by means of my baptism and confirmation I am called by Christ to serve his people by word and example.'

Figure 13.5 A congregation of shared responsibilities

One of the most significant developments in the way faith is expressed has been an understanding of the basic commitment made by all in the sacrament of baptism. What has been rediscovered is the experience upon which the understanding of our faith is built. In a parish of shared responsibilities, one way of expressing this sharing is to describe the willingness and naturalness of all Christians working together as a discovery of the personal responsibility for ministry which comes through the potential they have for more growth. 'In each one the Holy Spirit reveals His presence, giving something that is for the good of all' (1 Cor. 12.7).

Each person in the congregation begins to discover how they can offer themselves for service within the community of faith or in the wider world. They no longer see themselves as the helpers of the minister, or anyone else, but live with the joy of being called by Christ himself to work for the unfolding and realization of the kingdom wherever they are called to be. Jesus said to the Apostles, 'I no longer call you servants, but friends' (John 15.15).

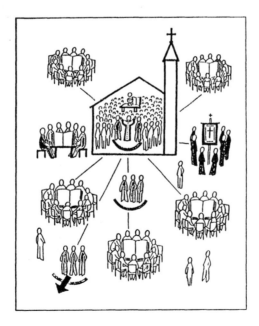

Figure 13.6 A congregation which is a community
of communities

The congregation is no longer a 'large group' of people but a living community which is being converted more and more into becoming the Body of Christ. Faith and life are shared in human-sized communities. In the discussion groups and the activity groups, the Word of God becomes the point of departure for Christian living.

The congregation is renewed, forming small Christian communities established as healthy cells. There is a pastoral, priestly role for the minister which far exceeds any concept which could have been dreamed of in the early stages of this development of sharing. Startling new discoveries have been made. In fact they are both old and new, since they embody the essential nature of the communities which became established in the early days of the sharing of the good news of the resurrection of Christ.

- In the only people of God, all the baptized, whether lay, religious or pastor, have essentially the same dignity and equality. No-one is more 'in the Church' than another. What is important is the service or ministry that is accomplished within it.
- First of all we are all brothers and sisters in baptism, then we are set apart by the specific mission to which we are called.
- Everyone is called by their baptism and confirmation to be Christian apostles, active, evangelical witnesses to Christ by their words and example.
- Everyone is called to the same 'vocation' of holiness.
- We are all called to live fully human lives as Christ's people.
- The same gospel guides everyone and makes the same demands. Only the paths are different.
- Everyone shares the same mission: to build or reveal something of the Kingdom of God.

Baptism and vocation

Our 'calling' or vocation to live responsibly as Christians has its root in our common baptism. It is this central understanding which is described in the introduction to what many feel was a ground-breaking document: the Church of England Board of Education report *All are Called: towards a theology of the laity* (1995). The introduction sets out the ways in which each of us needs to see our ministries as

- Priest
- Prophet
- King

⊳ All the baptized participate directly in the priesthood of Christ: 'You are a chosen race, a kingdom of priests, a consecrated nation, a people of God Chosen to be his and to proclaim his wonders' (1 Peter 2.9). Only the way of participating is different. Sometimes, in some denominations, we speak of the common priesthood of all the baptized and of the ministerial priesthood of the pastors of the Church.

⊳ A prophet is someone who speaks in the name of God, inspired by the gospel. Each true Christian is a prophet and can and must work jointly in evangelizing, primarily through the way in which they choose to order their lives.

⊳ All Christians are called to work for the enlarged realization of the Kingdom of God. This is begun in the family, at work and in the neighbourhood. The imprisonment of the kingdom is an attempt to restrict the description of God's activity to the ecclesiastical, social and domestic spheres of our lives. Christ the King is Lord of all the world and, as the Good Shepherd, cares for all its people.

Collaborative ministry, working as one body, can have a range of interpretations and it can look different according to local circumstances and denominational approaches. It does, however, have some basic underlying beliefs and requires a commitment on the part of those who work in this way to keep to them. In an inherently hierarchical denomination the work will be hard to put in place. In a denomination or congregation characterized by dependent relationships, many will be confused at first. In clergy-centred congregations tremendous learning will take place as new kinds of growth are experienced. From feeling undervalued and marginalized, clergy will come to see that they can hold the key to personal liberation and tremendous theological dialogue and learning. This concept of communion through community living will be rich food for the faithful and for the searcher.

Part III

Looking after yourself

14

Use your time well

Straight after Christmas dinner, Peter started work on the Lent course

Clergy of all kinds are a very precious resource for the churches. Every congregation needs a focus for its ministry and a person who will exercise appropriate leadership. So it is surprising that so little is done by any denomination to support clergy and provide developed programmes of in-service training. It is also a surprise, but more understandable, that many clergy do not plan out training for themselves as their ministry develops. They are one of the few professions which do not do this; indeed, it is hardly expected of them. There are no national programmes of clergy training. Dioceses provide organized 'induction' (or Post-Ordination) training for the first four years after ordination.

Post-Ordination Training

All bishops have an obligation to care for their clergy and a special responsibility to those who are newly ordained. This responsibility is usually delegated to a specially appointed person in the diocese, the Director of Training or of Post-Ordination Training. Deacons and priests meet together, or in their year groups, on a regular basis, usually every one or two months.

The programme for such 'Potty Training' will be a mixture of necessary informative sessions to bring new clergy up to date with the parochial and pastoral requirements of their work and specially designed sessions requested by the clergy group. These sessions will focus on the many issues of importance to these particular people, in the context of a diocese, or in the wider Church at that time. Some of this training will involve an interface with professionals in the secular world, where many similar skills are required and many common issues have to be faced. Specialist ministers will come and share their experience and visits may be arranged.

Alongside POT for new clergy, the Director of Training will normally organize events for training incumbents. Even if they have had several curates before, not all clergy have an understanding of the supervisory skills needed to train another person. Those who are having a curate for the first time need particular support. There are many occasions when the placement of a curate in a parish goes wrong. It is vital that both the incumbent and the curate know what is expected of them before they set out on this shared piece of training work. For both of them it is a fundamental exercise in ministerial development, in learning about themselves and their interpretation of priesthood in a parochial setting.

Self-help clergy support

'Find someone else to talk to.' This is the essence of any advice given in connection with clergy support. There are a number of ways in which clergy can find someone to talk to. Most frequently, a minister seeks out a colleague or someone they know to have supervisory or consultancy skills and finds time to meet with them in an organized and systematic way. Such one-to-one support is formally organized in some dioceses and has the official title of peer appraisal or peer review. Volunteers or, more properly, recommended individuals receive training in work review techniques from the diocese and these people are then matched with clergy who request such partnerships. On occasions groups of clergy do this for one another; this gives a different kind of support, but is still done among colleagues.

Hierarchical review

Every diocese now has a review scheme for its clergy, formerly known as appraisal but more often today called ministerial review. All bishops want to meet their clergy and discuss what is happening in their lives and their ministry. Organized schemes allow a bishop to spend individual time with clergy annually, or every two or three years. In dioceses with suffragan or area bishops, this work is often divided up. Many schemes which involve regular meetings with a bishop also include, in a different year, a meeting with an archdeacon. Often these meetings are more focused on the work in the parish.

Professionalism and priesthood

All ministerial review schemes and, to a large extent, POT programmes are voluntary. Clergy do not have to engage with them and some do not. Others feel that they belong very firmly to a 'party' grouping within the Church and take their training from that source.

There is only one 'ground rule' thing to say: all clergy are involved in supporting other people and giving various forms of advice, and this is not acceptable unless they are themselves voluntarily undertaking some supportive review of their own professional work. Many want to do this because they are concerned for their own development as ministers, deacons or priests. Others do it because they need to reflect on their place within the institution of the Church. They need some kind of objectivity and a way to distinguish themselves from their role. Yet others need work consultancy in order to understand what is happening within their

Church and how they can engage with change and renewal as an active part of their ministry.

In an article on 'Transformational Leadership' in the MODEM book, *Managing, Leading, Ministering*, Jayme Rolls has written about the need for review and renewal in any organization, and that this has a spiritual dimension:

> The largest organisations and consulting firms acknowledge that they do not fully understand how to bring human renewal into a workplace that is in dire need. We need information in pioneering and developing new ways of thinking about traditional models which can be achieved through a new spirituality of work and community. What will spur organisational change is an intersection of values of the sacred and the secular. This will involve developing a workplace spirituality characterised by service, authenticity, compassion, heroic action, courage and daring. It will require risk-taking, readiness, change agility, innovation, a broadened context of commitment to the greater good, connecting to stakeholder voice and transformational leadership. (p. 68)

Like all others in the caring and supportive professions, clergy need ministerial review. They need to be encouraged to join the schemes which are organized for them and to share their experiences of ministry with others. Openness and a willingness to accept vulnerability are an integral part of the priestly life. Those who try to develop this, however haltingly, will have a quality of life about them which encourages others to make more use of their often undervalued ministry.

Time off

Care for one's self begins with a life of balance. This equilibrium comes with appropriate amounts of work, time off, time for refreshment and time for stimulation and challenge.

No-one is completely effective if they give themselves to only one task. Other interests and parts of life can act as stimuli. We all know of instances where insights about a piece of work have come when we were away from the task or caught up in doing something different.

Advice about time off is not primarily about making our work-aholic side more effective. Time off, free, unclerical, non-work-focused time is necessary for us to continue to become more fully human. Time off is not primarily about self-indulgence. We need to give time to our families and our friends for their own sakes. They and we only continue to become more fully rounded as individuals if we give serious time to developing significant levels of relationship with one another.

Clergy need to make their time off public. Many parish-based clergy take one weekday off. This needs to be known to the congregation and church officers, undertakers and work colleagues – if not to the entire parish! Other clergy take time off when their partners and children get free time. School holidays, including half-terms, are important times for breaks. It is a responsibility for churchwardens, as well as for bishops, archdeacons and rural deans, to watch that clergy actually take the time off they say they will have.

Sabbatical study

There are occasions when a longer period of time needs to be taken away from any piece of work. Each denomination now has a rolling programme within which clergy can opt for sabbatical study leave for up to three months in the space of ten years or so of ministry. Budgeted money is set aside by dioceses for this. Clergy can also apply to charities for grant support.

Sabbatical leave is not just an extended holiday, though it should contain an element of this. It is study leave and needs to be planned. The worst kind of sabbatical is holiday plus a few things I really like doing. Valuable sabbatical leave is always planned with someone else, usually the Director of Ministerial Training. It needs to contain an element of travel, to experience the study topic in different cultural settings, and to be accompanied by some planned reading. At the end, sabbatical leave needs to be evaluated so that the minister involved can assess the learning and transformation which has taken place. Often this is done by submitting a piece of writing, or a video or some other visual presentation such as a picture or a sculpture. No-one going on sabbatical leave should want, or expect, to return as the same person, unchanged. Congregations should expect change. On return a minister needs to be able to describe to their congregation what they have been doing. If significant decisions for change have been made by the minister, these need to be negotiated in the relevant places.

DIY ministerial review preparation

A structured method of preparation can be a helpful lead into a review interview. It can also be useful as a private reflection on a retreat or quiet day. It can provide a perspective that brings out strengths and weaknesses. The following questionnaire can help with personal reflection and also bring out issues which can be explored in a peer or hierarchical review meeting.

1 Performance through time

- I rate my interest in my ministry 12 months ago as . . .
- My interest in my ministry now is . . .
- The amount of effort I put in 12 months ago was . . .
- The amount of effort I put into my ministry now is . . .
- My clarity of objectives 12 months ago was . . .
- My clarity of objectives is now . . .
- The confidence I had in performing my ministry 12 months ago was . . .
- I rate my confidence in performing my ministry now as . . .
- Did I feel my job was 'stretching' 12 months ago?
- Do I feel my job is 'stretching' now?
- My level of coping 12 months ago was . . .
- My level of coping now is . . .

2 How skills are felt to be valued

- How systematic am I?
- I describe my standard of administration as . . .
- I rate myself as a communicator as . . .
- I rate myself as an organizer as . . .
- I rate myself as a supervisor of staff as . . .
- My ability to delegate is . . .
- My skill in finding people to help me is . . .
- My ability to work with colleagues is . . .
- My interest in liturgy and service planning is . . .

- My interest in pastoral visiting is . . .
- My own willingness to ask for help is . . .
- My willingness or ability to receive new ideas is . . .

3 Personal attitudes and feelings about ministry

- Are my activities what my congregation seem to want?
- What gives me a feeling of affirmation in my ministry?
- Do I get feelings of loneliness in my ministry?
- Do I work hardest at the things I enjoy?
- Do I back away from the work I least enjoy?
- Do I attend meetings to be as positive as I can?
- Do I worry overmuch about what others think?
- Do I ever feel like leaving the job? Why?
- Is my family life enhanced by my ministry?
- Is my time-off as well-organized as my time-on?

4 Inner life and spirituality

- How disciplined is my prayer time?
- Do I have a spiritual director?
- How often do I make a retreat?
- What do I read?
- How often do I undertake any theological or skills training?
- What has been my experience of God recently?

5 Looking ahead

Where do I see myself:
- One year from now?
- Five years from now?
- Ten years from now?
- Does where I see myself coincide with where I hope to be?
- If retirement is on the horizon, what plans am I making?

What else would you want to ask yourself which is not in these questions?

Making training possible

It is part of the history of the Church that benefactors have left money in trust for the support of clergy and their families. Some of these funds are available for in-service training. The Director of Training in each diocese has details of what monies are available. The archdeacon and bishop will also often have access to charities. This money can be added to the annual in-service training allocation which each diocese makes for its clergy.

The use of time

All work in voluntary organizations, especially where there is no concept of nine-to-five about working hours, results in a sense of too much busyness. Clergy suffer from the 'workaholic' syndrome in a significant way. The disciplined use of a diary, with reflection on what its story tells, is important. This secular 'Twenty steps to successful time management' is a useful piece of self-reflection.

1 Clarify your objectives. Put them in writing. Then set your priorities. Make sure you are getting out of life what you really want.
2 Focus on objectives, not on activities. Your most important activities are those that help you to accomplish your objectives.
3 Set at least one major objective each day and achieve it.
4 Record a time log periodically to analyse how you use your time.
5 Analyse what you do, when you do it and why you do it. Ask yourself what would happen if you did not do it. Consider if you are the person who should be doing this.
6 Eliminate at least one time-wasting activity from your life each week.
7 Plan your time. Write out a plan for each week. Ask yourself what you hope to accomplish by the end of the week and what you will need to do to achieve these results.
8 Make a to-do list every day.
9 Plan your time each day to ensure you accomplish the most important things first.
10 Make sure that your first working hour is productive.

11 Set time limits for every task.
12 Take time to do it right the first time.
13 Eliminate recurring crises in your life. Find out why things keep going wrong. Learn to be proactive rather than reactive.
14 Make a quiet space in each day when you can review where you are with all your tasks.
15 Develop the habit of finishing what you start. Don't jump from one thing to another, leaving a string of unfinished tasks behind you.
16 Learn to do it now.
17 Resist your impulses to do unscheduled tasks, but allow time in a day for spontaneity and interruptions.
18 Never spend time on less important things when important ones are undone.
19 Take time for yourself, time to dream, time to relax, time to remember who you are.
20 Develop a personal philosophy of time – what time means to you and how time relates to your life.

Using a work consultant

None of us can understand what is going on in our lives without the aid of another person to reflect with. The use of a work consultant, in addition to a spiritual director, allows a structured analysis of your working life to be carried out. There are many people who are trained in this work. It is likely that the Director of Training in a diocese will have a number of names who can be suggested.

15

Power, conflict and service

Hilary found that Jean was wearing the same outfit

No minister or priest will get everything right in carrying out their work. With hindsight many will say that they are glad they did not know all they would have to go through and that at times the experience was like tiptoeing through a minefield. I once went to a concert where the choir president said the performance had only been so very good because there had been so many disasters on the way!

All of us face questions about Christian ministry using different levels of understanding. At one level change happens when we are unable to carry on life as before. Every week, clergy have thousands of different pastoral encounters with parishioners and those they work with. Some of these occasions are going to have tense moments. It is inevitable that there will be friction in working relationships and occasionally some difference of opinion. 'What is done cannot be undone.' At another level argument and disagreement are about putting things right or making organizational adjustments in a place or a congregation where things are not being done as effectively as they might. More deeply, approaches to any difficulty can be transformed, and our intransigence and mistaken attitudes redeemed, if the Christian concept of service or servanthood runs through our attitudes and our actions.

The use of power

Unequal relationships

Strong advice from those with whom I have discussed this chapter leads me to begin with a section on bullying. Many people, not least junior clergy and women priests, have told me that this is one difficult aspect of working relationships which they experience.

It is a truism to say that the Church as it has developed can hardly be recognized in the intentions of Jesus of Nazareth and the relationships he established with those who came to him. The word hierarchy came into general usage from its origins in ecclesiastical structures. Episcopally-led churches, at the least, derive their structure from an order of society in Roman and medieval times. Such churches mirror to some extent the early concepts of a society with different strata and severe social divisions. Its system of preferment still depends on patronage and the choices of the few and is in no way open and competitive.

Within this structure many say that they have been made to feel very 'junior' or that they feel that they are 'outsiders' in a system which appears unable or unwilling to let them in. Very many clergy say that they experience a 'glass ceiling' about appointments. Women priests in some dioceses say that they experience this sense of exclusion more strongly than male priests.

'Bullying' is not an easy term and there can be little more than anecdotal evidence to support its existence in the Church. It has its origins in an imbalance of relationships and an inappropriate use of power. On many occasions clergy seem to use their position to get their way rather than choosing to enter into dialogue with those who see things differently.

The churches, even in the reformed tradition, are not always places where free and open debate leads to guidance from the Holy Spirit. There are denominations where church leaders are accountable and where office is held for a limited period of time. In others, particularly the episcopally-led churches, there is little accountability and offices can be held from appointment to retirement. This tremendous security, hardly given to any other profession nowadays, can lead to assumptions about authority which are not always fully explained and to attitudes towards junior clergy which are experienced by them as oppressive. Communication, a sense of humility at the privilege of office and an ability to apologize are areas which church leaders need to be reminded to visit perhaps more often than others. I will develop a contemporary theme of 'servant leadership' at the end of this chapter, but before that it is important to explore the areas in the working situations of clergy where conflict is likely to arise. A heightened awareness of these can help some to be avoided and others to be resolved.

Common sources of conflict

People disagree about values and beliefs

Congregations disagree about what the Church is and what it ought to be about. Such disagreement means that the vision of the Church is unclear. Consequently the congregation will not have worked out its goals or objectives. If statements have been made in everyone's name without their real consent there will be frustration when little action results from them.

The way through this is to spend much more time than the enthusiasts would like in consulting and listening to all those involved. Only when most people feel that opinions have been heard, if not necessarily acted on, will the reluctant come along and ownership be felt by almost everyone.

The structures are unclear

In churches and congregations without clear structures no-one is sure what to do and no-one is sure what anyone else is supposed to do. There are no understood agreements or guidelines about the roles and responsibilities of clergy, staff, lay people or church committees. This lack of clarity is a constant source of conflict. Because no-one is sure what to do, either nothing gets done because no-one will take responsibility or nothing seems to be achieved because one group or person will continually challenge the activity of the others. I was once asked to spend time with a congregation where the meetings were adequate but nothing happened afterwards. When I sat in on the meetings, I soon discovered that clear decisions could not be made in many cases because there was insufficient information available on which to make a decision. On other occasions, at the end of what seemed like a productive discussion, the question, 'So who will take responsibility for this?' was never asked. At best it was assumed that the vicar would pick up this responsibility. When nothing had happened by the next meeting anger and frustration frequently resulted.

Structures can also be obscured or invalidated in congregations where one group continually disregards the agreed way of doing things. People who are unwilling to work within an agreed structure can be influential and visionary; they can also enjoy the frustration and confusion caused by their actions.

One way forward is for lines of accountability to be made clear and for those who have executive authority to act responsibly and use the powers given to them to keep people and groups within agreed structures and courses of action. This is not a recommendation for stultifying bureaucracy but a recognition that carefully worked out and agreed structures can enable change as well as prevent it. As churches grow they will need agreed structures more and more. Even small and family-sized congregations need to have structures which are in place, understood and respected.

The structures no longer fit the size of the congregation

Increases in numbers can be a great source of joy. It is what most congregations say that they want. However, a change in size can also be a source of trouble and conflict. A congregation which is growing, or shrinking, often finds itself operating in a way that is inappropriate for its present size. If a congregation is smaller than it used to be, it often tries to operate as it did in the past. It will have too many committees and activities which .put a tremendous strain on the remaining number of willing people. It is often helpful for an outsider, or a senior member of the denomination, to come in and act as a consultant to rationalize a situation which those within it are unable to face.

In churches which are growing, a different situation obtains. There is a well-remembered time 'when everybody knew everybody and the minister was able to call'. Now life within the congregation is more likely to take place in small groups and tasks are carried out by members who are not well known to everyone. The minister is surrounded by an overwhelming set of expectations. An appropriate way forward here is to have occasional times when all the congregation are able to meet together and socialize, meet newcomers and negotiate the expectations put on leaders. There needs to be a celebration of the growth which has taken place and some measure of consensus that if growth is to continue, then people, and that includes the minister, will have to act in different ways – both to survive and to make the whole ministry of the congregation effective.

Clergy and parish styles are in conflict

Congregations which are in trouble often try to focus the problem on the style of ministry of the priest. Clergy relate to congregations in very different ways. What is most crucial is for the right kind of minister to come to a congregation at the right time in its life. Clergy who are very active are right for times of growth and change. They will not fit will into a congregation which needs consolidation after a rapid time of change. Extremely pastoral, person-centred clergy will do well at times when congregations need to be nursed or when previous troubles need to be healed. They will be resented if the appropriate style needed for that phase is a person who will grasp nettles, 'see the trouble-makers off' and establish new working practices.

Conflict which is not brought on by a new minister can arise where he or she is following a priest who had stayed a very long time. Surprisingly large numbers of such new ministers do not remain long in post. This is either because a congregation is still grieving the loss of the last minister or because that person's style of ministry has become so ingrained that only years of patient listening and encouragement will avoid an explosion or turn a congregation from terminal grieving decline.

The new minister rushes into changes

All congregations are both keen to welcome their new minister and anxious about what changes will be made. Many clergy arriving in their new situations do not take enough time to get to know their people before rushing to make changes. Frequently, these changes are not enormous and shocking; they are tiny things brought in without explanation. Most members of a congregation are reluctant to ask a minister why changes are being made. Some changes are unwitting; a minister is simply doing what they have always done, or have brought a practice they liked from their previous congregation. It will feel like continuity and familiarity to them but will appear as change and innovation to the new congregation.

Visiting, talking, explaining and questioning will go some way to overcoming this, as will asking people what they like about new practices where difference is voiced. The minister who introduces the Peace to a communion service and walks around sharing it in a congregation unfamiliar with the practice will be brave and liberating to some or, more likely, bruised and blamed by many!

Change can best be brought about by the minister who has developed the necessary level of trust and understanding with a congregation and been able to involve others in the decisions and actions which are needed to bring about change.

Lines of communication are blocked

It is easy to blame problems in a congregation on loss of communication or on bad communication. Often communication problems are more the *result* of conflict than the cause of it.

When conflict arises or escalates, members of one faction or group tend to try to avoid contact or communication with others. Steps need to be taken to prevent conflict hardening and attempts made to exaggerate difference and create scapegoats.

Often, in a troubled congregation, the minister and church council think that by withholding information they are helping to diffuse a situation. In fact, they are allowing distortions to grow and are creating a vacuum where false rumours can sprout.

One very good way to take the tension out of a situation is to offer 'open forum' meetings, perhaps facilitated by an outsider, where a balance of feelings and opinions can be expressed in a structured and controlled way. If people can meet face-to-face it is much more difficult to maintain absolute positions and it is possible to begin shared discussions about ways forward. Those who stay away from such consultations become marginalized and either leave or try to find a face-saving way back in. Here a consultant or sensitive minister can be a great asset.

People manage conflict badly

Very many churchpeople hold the unspoken view that conflict is bad and should not be acknowledged or allowed to happen: 'Even if conflict is there we will not recognize it.' The best response is to try to be realistic and face the facts of a situation.

- Conflict is a part of everyday life and is neither good nor bad in itself.
- Conflict creates the energy which makes change possible.
- Conflict only becomes destructive when it is mismanaged.
- Well managed conflict is hardly recognized as such; it is experienced as a release of energy.
- Conflict which is resolved by negotiation is often experienced as a 'win-win' situation where both or all sides feel that they have gained something without giving away anything vital and without an awkward compromise of principle.
- When conflict is denied, so also is the opportunity to deal with it in constructive ways.
- Avoidance of conflict causes 'triangling', where a third person is told about a situation and invited to sympathize or collude.
- When conflict is denied, anger is not released; it becomes embittering and inwardly destructive.

Disaffected members hold back resources

Change causes people to want to hold on to what is seen by them as security. This becomes particularly apparent when those who control a group or an area of finance will not let go. It is equally significant when a person is responsible for a part of the church building or the hall. They will try to control their physical territory to prevent change making any progress. This strategy is not exclusively the territory of the church organist or the hall caretaker – but they could teach courses on it!

Care, patience, explanations and, occasionally, firmness which will allow a gracious climb-down are a very good way forward. Unfortunately, the disaffected, like the poor in Our Lord's phrase, will always be with us. They have a rightful place in any caring and collaborative community, a right to be heard but not a right to prevent change or to subvert planning exercised with integrity.

Tension, uncertainty and conflict

The most significant thread running through all accounts of the causes of conflict is change and uncertainty about the future. Change not only takes place within a congregation and causes anxiety; it also takes place in the relationship of a congregation to its environment – the community in which it is placed and the wider world which is perceived as either indifferent or apathetic, made up of Christians who express their faith in very different ways and of members of other faiths who appear to have a much deeper, even aggressive commitment to the whole culture which surrounds belief.

New ways of responding to conflict and change are emerging. These differences have been well described by Professor Gillian Stamp in an essay entitled *The Enhancement of Ministry in Uncertainty* (Brunel Institute of Organization and Social Studies, 1993). She says that, in her experience, when organizations are used to working together to bring about change, even in collaborative ways, they expect that once they have adapted to a new set of circumstances things will 'settle down' again to the kind of equilibrium which they had previously enjoyed. Her observations are that organizations today are no longer 'making changes' and expecting 'things to calm down again'. They seem to be saying that 'the only thing we can be certain of these days is uncertainty'. A way of maximizing this realization, rather than seeing it as a deeply pessimistic observation, is to try to work with the forces of change instead of taking massive stances to resist. For churches this approach has led to considerable controversy. If they seem to be going too much with 'the spirit of the age', then they are accused of either trendiness, relevance or following moral or intellectual fashion. On the other hand, a stubborn defensiveness frequently results in an unwillingness to engage with the ideas and controversies of a changing society and Church and a fossilization of organization, belief and structures.

Living with uncertainty and provisionality is, after all, a biblical concept. The 'heroes' of the Old Testament – Moses, Abraham, David and any number of the prophets – moved on in faith to changing circumstances and felt led to do so because of their trust in God. The whole experience of exile and of self-understanding as 'the remnant' meant that a people and a community of faith had to look at itself again and ask what God was saying in situations of forced change. Jesus continually felt the need to move on. It is a widely held view that the progress of his ministry led Jesus on into deeper situations of conflict until things came to a climax in the last week of his life in Jerusalem. The disciples and followers of Jesus left their own security and followed him in his itinerant ministry. After his resurrection the newly forming Church was continually beset by tensions, conflicts and change as the Apostles and the newly-converted Christians faced expansion. For many people it seems that the churches are coming to the end of many centuries of settled, cautious conservatism. The atmosphere of many renewed but still small churches seems more like that of the young churches of the first centuries. Change is being forced by numerical decline, a re-evaluation of the way belief is expressed, and pressure from growing churches in developing countries which demonstrate that growth and a vibrant faith only begin when the old structures and support systems are swept away.

Problem solving and uncertainty

Perhaps the most difficult part of life for clergy is when tension pervades a situation. There will always be difficult people in congregations and they will always be wearing on nervous energy. If it is possible to distance one's self from a problem, or the people involved in it, then perspective and some objectivity can be gained. When I worked with Avec we used this 'Problem solving sequence', devised by Dr George Lovell and Miss Catherine Widdicombe and adapted by the Revd Peter Russell.

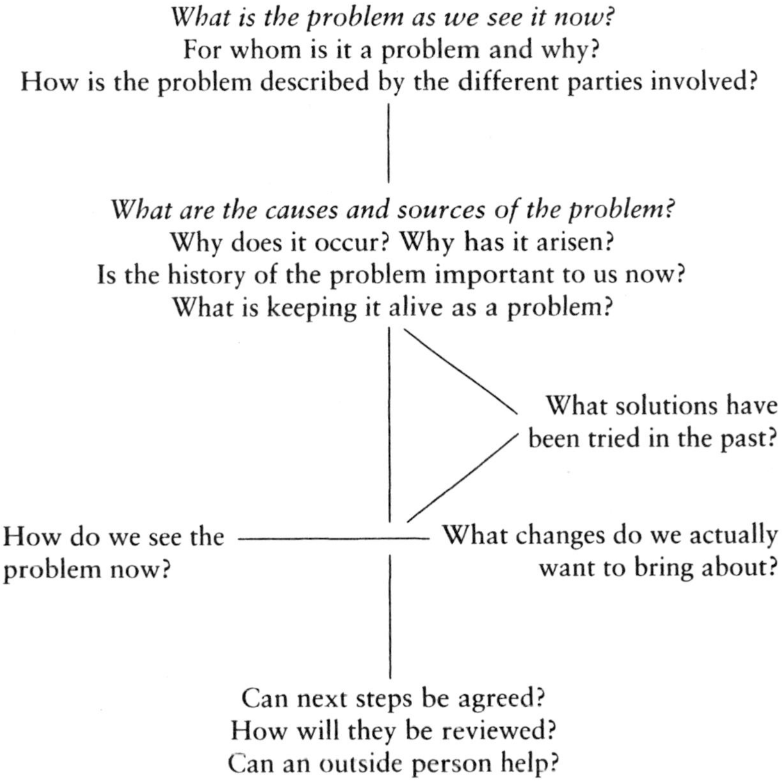

What is the problem as we see it now?
For whom is it a problem and why?
How is the problem described by the different parties involved?

What are the causes and sources of the problem?
Why does it occur? Why has it arisen?
Is the history of the problem important to us now?
What is keeping it alive as a problem?

What solutions have
been tried in the past?

How do we see the ———— What changes do we actually
problem now?   want to bring about?

Can next steps be agreed?
How will they be reviewed?
Can an outside person help?

Figure 15.1 The problem solving sequence

Conflict and a ministry of service

How can there be conflict in a church built on the foundation of
humility and service? The idea of servanthood is deeply embedded
in both our Christian culture and our inherited Englishness. It is also
a basic theological and ministerial concept. For many Christians,
especially around the Easter season, the vision of the 'suffering
servant' appears in our religious consciousness. The prophet Isaiah
described the idea of a servant suffering on behalf of others (Chapter 53) and this was picked up and used by Jesus and those who
interpreted the significance of his death in the life of the Church.
The importance of this key gospel concept is that it is God who

initiates the one act of redemptive self-offering which is performed by the Servant-Messiah.

Above all others, this idea of redemptive self-sacrifice is what brings many to the life and person of Jesus. Describing him as 'the man for others' communicates to believer and non-believer at a very deep level. It should come as no surprise, then, that a way of understanding the life of a congregation should follow this approach to action. Particularly in times of stress and transition, it is the willingness to give oneself in listening and service to others which will bring about redemptive change. This level of spiritual understanding will transcend working methods of collaboration. In a society which has gravitated to self-protection and to aims of self-fulfilment even in spiritual journeying, the refreshing willingness of self-giving can really make the life of a congregation a model way, if at times misunderstood by the wider community. This is much more than community service and helping others; it is a willingness to give up and give away which looks like weakness and vulnerability to those who do not want to see.

The servant ministry, if it can be called that, is a part of English culture. Government ministers are called 'civil servants'; government offices are 'ministries'. Even if obscured by over-familiarity, these public titles are a constant and timely reminder of how people and groups might relate to one another. They stem from the biblical tradition. More significantly, the whole idea of service is summed up in the word 'diaconia'. It is not surprising, therefore, that the concept of Christian disciples as ministers/servants should have received great emphasis in the early Church and been carried on right up to the present day. As a consequence of Christian baptism it has always been understood that there are no 'lay' members in the Church without a ministry within it. The central way of working out a ministry is through servanthood, just as Christ saw himself as a servant, giving himself for others. The development of a special order of the diaconate within the Church should not allow this basic idea to be overshadowed. Equally, bishops and priests should never forget that they were first ordained as deacons and deacons they remain. Christ himself reminded his disciples in that when they offer deeds of service to another person in need, they are serving him.

Service and willingness to serve

In times of crisis and change it is all too easy to retreat into defensive positions and 'pull up the drawbridge'. No amount of analysis about what is going on in a congregation will make any difference if its clergy are not, at a simple and basic level, prepared to live and minister in a 'Christ-like' way. The essence of that way is to be prepared to approach one another in the form of a servant ministry. By doing this, those who wish can see the image of what God was doing in Christ in our actions and attitudes. How else can we dare to call ourselves his Body other than as people broken in the service of others?

16

Spirituality and a Rule of Life

**For his spiritual exercises, Frank used the Anglican
cycle of prayer**

I hate routine. There is nothing worse for me than doing the same
thing on the same day each week. Perhaps this stems from the time
in my childhood when we visited the same aunt every Saturday
evening and, in post-war days, had much the same for Sunday tea
each week. In another way I know that I am a creature of habit
with my own rituals. Up to breakfast time each day my wife and
I know who makes the tea, who sets the breakfast and which order
for the shower!

Spirituality for clergy: a Rule of Life

There is an idea, honoured as much in the breach as in the observance, that clergy say morning and evening Offices each working day. Some do, and they are to be commended for it. But the life of very many clergy means that they cannot have such an ordered regime. Busyness, the need to attend meetings, even the collection of children from school, mean that regular daytime patterns of prayer get interrupted. Yet at the heart of every priest, as of every Christian person, there does need to be a worked-out pattern which enables prayers to be said. The time-honoured way of achieving this is by developing a Rule of Life.

We all know many others for whom life is a set pattern, out of choice or otherwise. The same bus or train each day for work, the same supermarket for shopping on the same day, the school run, the club, the hobby, or the evening class. Even the same time for church, the same seat, the same role and duties year in and year out. Working as I do in the locality of Haworth, I have a perpetual fear of a life like that of the Revd Patrick Brontë, who retired to bed at the same time every evening, pausing half way up the stairs to rewind the grandfather clock! I am consoled by the thought that after he had gone the children were free to give full rein to their imaginations in the sitting room downstairs, composing the most inventive stories in a language all of their own.

So it is with some personal horror that I come to propose and discuss the importance of any kind of set of rules and regulations to help clergy lead an ordered and structured spiritual life. Perhaps the most helpful first step in such an exploration is to look at what the word and concept of 'a Rule of Life' might mean, before I begin an exploration of its content or analyse why many of us react against complying with a set of rules or an ordered system of any kind.

In spiritual direction terms, the word 'rule' has the meaning of 'measure' or 'regulation'. This use comes from the Greek and Latin languages. In Greek the word is translated as 'canon', and used in the same way as scriptural books are 'measured' to see if they come up to a certain standard for inclusion in the Old or New Testaments. In Latin the word 'regula' is translated as 'rule, pattern, model, or example'. From these words, and their use, living by a 'Rule' is more about living a regular, 'ordered' life which tries to work towards a certain standard, after the model or pattern of Jesus or of one of the saints who have followed him.

Do it yourself or a given Rule of Life?

Harold Miller, in a Grove Booklet entitled *Finding a Personal Rule of Life*, lists the advantages of a given Rule of Life as follows:

- A given Rule may well have a balance which our own personal devising (even in conjunction with others) will not have. It may also be much more obviously in line with a Christian tradition.
- A given Rule may be particularly useful for those who are indecisive.
- There are some people who find it preferable to be required to adjust themselves, rather than have the freedom to adjust the Rule. (p. 12)

Devising your own Rule

The construction of any such personal discipline cannot be done alone. If we try it, we fail. There is no external reference point. Time pushes out our best intentions. Our needs in spiritual development may change – they must change if we are in a continual process of formation. It is, therefore, *essential* that a Rule is put together and reviewed with someone else. Friends, Christian friends, are most probably available for this, and there are spiritual guides and directors to support and help. Many clergy can do this. In the end the appropriate nickname of 'Soul Friend' will and should describe the person you are looking for (see *Soul Friend* by Kenneth Leech).

Understanding the concept of a Rule of Life also has to come up to the 'measure' of how a New Testament faith is understood. This is not a life lived under the rigorous and unforgiving eye of a legalistic scheme, worshipping a law-bound God. It is a rule freely accepted, which tries to live life to a certain standard with a set of bench marks and personal disciplines. For the Christian this is a life lived with a growing sense of God's forgiveness and the graciousness we experience as we are being upheld. It follows an understanding of the life and death of Jesus which allows us now to live lives dedicated to following him, lives born of charity and freedom and not of punishment and law.

In search of the self

Any reflection on keeping a Rule of Life and clergy reactions to it needs to include some exploration of our motives and our understandings of our self. There is a very strong sense that if we are to 'take Christianity seriously' then we must take a route of exploration which involves learning about the tradition and exploring our reactions to it and to how it might impact on our personal and everyday lives. If we are to develop an understanding of this faith and if we are going to set the standards for life after the example of God in Jesus, then we need to know why we respond positively to some things in religion and react in a negative way to others. It will help in approaching the question of keeping a Rule of Life to know why we react against rules and regulations and the idea of a regular pattern of prayer, while at other times in our everyday lives we depend on regularity and ritual.

The best modern way to explain this search for understandings of self is to describe the exploration as a 'journey inwards'. For many in our Western society our identity is characterized by a sense of 'inwardness'. We understand ourselves as people who have a set of complex states and emotions which lie deep within ourselves. We have come to think that the further inwards we go to our own consciousness, the more we shall understand about ourselves. We have also come to think that we have a dark and mysterious unconscious which influences how we behave and which is inaccessible to our conscious mind.

Spiritual direction and personality indicators

In trying to understand ourselves and our reactions to certain situations, as well as to other people, it is the Myers-Briggs Type Indicators which Christian people (and many others) use today. Katherine Briggs and her daughter, Isabel Briggs Myers, used the work of Carl Jung to establish an analysis of personality into a series of types. Jung thought that the human psyche is composed of numerous parts, including the surface, conscious 'persona' which we show to the world and a hidden 'shadow' that we hide from the world and frequently also from ourselves. The conclusion of Jung's process of self-discovery and self-acceptance is the emergence from our unconscious depths of our real identity, something which he calls the archetype of the 'Self'. This concept or discovery is closely related to what Jung calls 'God'. Indeed he is reluctant to speak of a God who might exist independently of the Self.

Katherine Briggs became fascinated by the similarities and differences between people and personality. She discovered that Jung had developed a system of types and she began to explore and elaborate on these. Isabel worked with her mother and developed a means of measuring and quantifying personality types. Jung's primary distinction was between extrovert and introvert types. His theory was that extroversion (E) derives from the direction of a person's energy outwards towards others, while introversion (I) results from the direction of energy inwards towards the self. While many Christians would not necessarily allow this distinction to be determinative, it is agreed, particularly in the Myers-Briggs Indicator analysis, to be a helpful guide to personality. Many trainers and work consultants use this as a way into the debate about how relationships are formed in teams and work groups. The idea of 'shadow' and its use in a development of these indicators helps with an exploration and understanding of what we hide from the world and often also from ourselves. These are on the whole secular tools, but they have a deep personal, psychological and spiritual resonance. The whole concept of a 'journey inwards' and a 'journey outwards' is important in any spiritual understanding, and in the design of a Rule of Life.

Christian formation

What has now become established, as much in spiritual direction as in adult education, is the importance of the concept of spiritual formation and re-formation as a lifelong process. It can almost be described as growth towards the person God wants us to be. It was the most important concept to be proposed and introduced when I conducted a review of the Third Order of the Society of St Francis. The same idea – that our process of spiritual development is lifelong – needs to characterize any piece of spirituality planning and all schemes, programmes or rules following any particular spiritual tradition. What is put into a Rule of Life depends on the source of any spiritual teaching or construction. These can range from a time of Bible reading and silence, a 'quiet time' at the beginning or end of the day, to the following of a scheme which originates from one of the great spiritual teachers such as St Benedict or St Ignatius. In this exploration we shall look at the ways of prayer and self-discipline which originate from St Francis. I want to use the *Principles of the Third Order* as a suggested basis for the construction of a Rule of Life.

A Bible-based rule

The beginning of any attempt at a rule for a Christian is the teaching and example of Christ. The life and, particularly, the death of Jesus are the great example of his own sacrifice. The Third Order of St Francis has a simple way of setting out a rule and I want to commend it here for clergy as well as lay people. The rule is broken up into sections and actions. I have given them the headings of Vocation, Ministry and Fruitfulness.

Vocation

In the first concept, that of Vocation, there are three tasks.

1 To make Our Lord known and loved everywhere
There is a demand on those who have grasped something of the quality of life and nature of the sacrifice, death and resurrection of Jesus to make this discovery known to others in any appropriate way.

> The primary aim is to make Christ known. This is the obedience which the gospel lays upon us all which, shaping our lives and attitudes, will reflect the obedience of those whom the Lord chose to be with him and whom he sent forth as his witnesses.

2 To spread the spirit of community
As an immediate consequence of faith, there is a demand on all Christians to share a vision of how men and women could live together in community.

> We should accept, then, as a second aim the spreading of community amongst all people. We are pledged to fight against all

the ignorance, pride and prejudice which breed injustice or partiality on account of distinctions of race, sex, colour, class or caste, creed, status or education. They will combat such injustice in the name of Christ their master, in whom there can be neither Jew nor Greek, bond nor free, male nor female; for in him all are one.

3 To live simply

One of the greatest issues of our day for Christians who live in the developed and therefore rich world is that of lifestyle.

Tertiaries, though they possess property and earn money to support themselves and their families, show themselves true followers of Christ and of St Francis by their readiness to live simply and to share with others. They recognise that some of their members may be called to a literal following of St Francis in a life of extreme simplicity. All, however, accept that they avoid luxury and waste, and regard their possessions as being held in trust for God. . . . Tertiaries are concerned more for the generosity that gives all, rather than the value of poverty in itself. In this way they reflect in spirit the acceptance of Jesus' challenge to sell all, give to the poor, and follow him.

It is interesting that, in the scheme set out by Francis for his followers, the vision of faith and a world which reflects the kingdom comes first. Now, secondly, come the ways to bring it about.

Ministry

In the second injunction, that of Ministry, there are three ways of service.

1 Prayer

There is no weapon more potent than the prayer of intercession for furthering the purposes of Christ's kingdom. Some who have much time will be able to give to prayer a large place in their daily lives, but even those for whom this is impossible must not fail to recognise its primary importance and will guard carefully from interruption such time as they have allotted to it. The heart of prayer is the Eucharist, in which with their fellow Christians and in union with their Lord and Saviour in his sacrifice is renewed and deepened as they make again memorial before God of his death and passion, and feed upon his sacrificial life.

2 Study

Study is of the scriptures first of all, followed by commentaries on them and the use of aids to prayer and devotion.

> The true knowledge is the knowledge of God. The first place will be given to devotional study of the scriptures as one of the chief means of attaining that knowledge of God which leads to eternal life. In addition [Tertiaries] should recognise the Christian responsibility for pursuing other branches of study, both sacred and secular; and in particular there should be those who accept the duty of forwarding its special aims, by contributing through their researches and writings to a better understanding of the church's world-wide mission, of the application of Christian principles to the use and distribution of wealth, and of all issues that pertain to human community.

3 Work

The purpose of the Christian life is to undertake work which will reflect and further the kingdom. One of the principal characteristics of this work will be a ministry of service.

> Jesus the master took on himself the form of a servant. He came 'not to be ministered unto but to minister'. He went about doing good, healing the sick, preaching good tidings to the poor and binding up the broken-hearted . . . Lives will be marked throughout by a reflection of the One who came among us as servant of all. The chief form of service which can be offered is to reflect the love of God, who, in his beauty and power, is the inspiration and joy of our own lives.

Much has been written about Servant Ministry in recent times, not without some controversy (see, for example, Robert K. Greenleaf's *Servant Ministry*). Jesus himself seems to have made the concept central to his own life and work. But the man who washed the disciples' feet was also a man of great courage and strength of character. Service is not a 'wet' approach to life. Humility may well take greater courage than some more high profile and assertive courses of action.

Fruitfulness

The third concept, fruitfulness, also has three aspects. Franciscans and Tertiaries talk of the Notes of their Order, which I interpret as 'fruits of the spirit' for all Christians. They are Humility, Love and Joy.

1 Humility

Humility confesses that we have nothing that we have not received and admits the fact of our insufficiency and dependence upon God. It is the mother of all Christian virtues. It is the first condition of a happy life within any house or fellowship.

2 Love

The master says: 'by this shall all men know that ye are my disciples, if ye love one another'. Love is thus the distinguishing feature of all true disciples of Christ. God is love and for those whose lives are hid with Christ in God, love will be the very atmosphere that surrounds all they do.

3 Joy

[Tertiaries] rejoicing in the Lord always, will show forth in their lives the grace and beauty of divine joy. They will remember that they follow the Son of Man, who came eating and drinking, who loved the birds and flowers, who blessed the little children, who was the friend of publicans and sinners, who sat at the tables alike of the rich and the poor. They will therefore cast off all gloom and moroseness, all undue aloofness from the common interests of men, and will delight in laughter and good fellowship. They will rejoice in God's world, its beauty and its living creatures, calling nothing clean or unclean. They will mingle freely with all kinds of people, ready to bind up the broken-hearted and to bring good cheer into other lives. They will carry with them an inner happiness and peace which all may feel even if they do not guess its source.

The humility, love and joy which should mark the lives of all Christians are supernatural graces which can be won only from the Divine Bounty: they can never be obtained by unaided human exertion. They are miraculous gifts of the Holy Ghost. Yet it is the purpose of Christ to work miracles through us, and if we his servants will but be emptied of self and utterly surrendered to him, we will become chosen vessels of his mighty working, who is able to do exceedingly abundantly, above all that we may ask or think.

(The extracts are taken, with very little adaptation, from *The Principles of the Third Order*. They are probably being revised to incorporate inclusive language and a more recent Bible translation as I write.)

Being and doing

For each of us the importance of establishing a Rule of Life is that it makes us begin our personal journey and our spiritual exploration of God. It insists that we begin to establish lives of prayer, with silence, study and reflection, before we rush into the activity of either applying what we have discovered or trying to share the faith with others by word or deed.

Using a spiritual director

A spiritual director should be someone who

- is ready to listen to you, whatever you have to say, with sympathetic, concentrated attention and will never be shocked;
- does not immediately respond with ever-ready good advice or accounts of their own experiences but asks questions which cause you, yourself, to look more deeply or in a different way, at what you have revealed;
- can be trusted to keep the information you have given them confidential, resisting all temptation to share anything that you have said, except in certain previously agreed circumstances.

Personal responsibility

Certain pointers emerge from the material which has been explored in this chapter. These may help you to set out on that all-important further journey of spiritual growth and development.

➪ No-one can construct a Rule of Life for you.
➪ The demands of a rule are structure and self-discipline.
➪ There are many patterns for a rule which you may be led to follow.
➪ Your temperament and church tradition will lead you towards some structures and away from others.
➪ The development of your inner life and spirituality comes before Christian action but goes alongside it.
➪ Lifelong formation, like lifelong learning, is for the whole of the Christian journey.

A rule is a measure – in modern language, a reviewable achievement – of how you are progressing.

Formation and the Christian life

The real enquiry and adventure is to launch out and try to use a Rule of Life for yourself. 'Formation' also gives you the three words which will launch you and keep you on your journey. *Information* will show you how to begin and how to bring in other resources. *Confirmation* will bring you within this rich tradition which is the Christian faith. The lifelong journey of formation will, in an imperceptible way, lead to our *Transformation*. As we become more Christ-like we have within ourselves something which is of immense value. It will place us in a particular and personal relation to Jesus Christ and the world he came to redeem. It will keep us within the Church of Christ which each generation is required to *re-form* and rebuild.

17

Lifestyle

'And I bet he does 1662,' sneered Clarence

The most difficult thing for clergy, their families and their friends to understand is clergy lifestyle in the Church of today. Who are these people who have chosen to become vicars? Are they monks or nuns with a liberalized lifestyle? Are they really just like lay people but with a special role in society? How much do their life choices affect their families? Is being a vicar a job for life or just until retirement? Does it entail giving up the freedoms, even to follow God in different ways, which other people have? Must the large, different, awkward house go with the job? Should they wear that dog collar all the time, just when at 'work', or only when taking services? Confusing, isn't it? This is the time to bring into the open many of the tensions and confusions, as well as the disciplines or obligations, which go with clergywork and clergylife.

Money

Clergy are not rich. They can never be so with the relatively small stipend which they receive. Many people these days take a significant drop in their own income when they are ordained or go to college. Many more lose an enormous slice of the family income if the ordained one moves parishes or jobs and the non-ordained partner has to give up their high earning position. Many clergy families now are sustained more by the income of the non-clergy partner. If they are a professional in some other sphere, their earnings can be more than double that of the clergyperson.

In almost every family a lower level of income is freely accepted, though resentment can easily come to the surface when things go wrong or when family tensions emerge. The issue which needs to be considered here is that money and conditions are rarely made explicit at the time of training – or at any other time. I do not want to raise the question as one which is necessarily full of problems. The vast majority of clergy homes are enjoyable places. Clergy families produce an astonishingly high proportion of children with significant achievements in public service, the professions, academia and the world of media and entertainment. The interesting question is how, in a world of financial- and possession-driven success, a lifestyle can emerge from our vicarages which can be an enhancing discovery.

There can be a way of life which does not depend on high earnings, luxury goods and expensive holidays. The days have gone when clergy families depended on jumble sales for clothing and charity grants and handouts from parishioners were a demeaning part of clergy life. Now clergy live in a culture of mutual dependence. The diocese, through the giving of congregations and from its historic resources, maintains the house free of rent and rates. The Church Commissioners still (struggle to) maintain a non-contributory pension scheme. In return clergy are readily available, except for agreed time off. They choose to uphold negotiated conventions about behaviour and relationships within the parish and become a part of the public fabric of English life.

All of this is at a cost which balances the privileges. The 'clericalism' which develops around a clergy lifestyle is sometimes felt to be at the cost of individualism and identity. The public role, with its 'caricature' identity, can take over and submerge real personality. Alternatively, clericalism can give full rein to idiosyncrasy and allow the extrovert or the weak personality to hide behind a role. The privileges are many. Clergy can go where few others are allowed. They receive intimacies which are the greatest privilege. They can preside at the most special, public or private family occasions. All of this goes to make up the astonishing collage which is a clergy lifestyle. Within it there are many choices to be made and this chapter needs to explore many of them.

Family finances

The finances of a clergy home need to be managed very carefully. I am aware of the worldliness of this seemingly sound and sensible piece of advice, and it needs to be balanced with the teaching that a lack of care for money and worldly goods should be part of the lifestyle of every Christian. This is right, and an over-dependence on goods, possessions and the trappings of wealth should not be a characteristic of the clergy lifestyle.

What I am advocating is the sensible stewardship of what is given to a clergy family, and an awareness of the limitations and opportunities of the money available. Clergy do need to take professional advice about their finances. As notional, but actually, self-employed people they may have to cope with the Inland Revenue self-assessment tax return. If there is extra money coming in, there is an extra need to record it and pay any tax liable. Dealing with large amounts of unpaid tax can be complicated, and professional advice can help with planned payments – and get some back as rebates where overpayments have been made.

Housing

Living in a vicarage is not the same as having a home of your own. While decorating is normally done adequately in parsonage houses and gardens are well kept, there is something different about doing this to your own home. As many of those now being ordained come into this clerical life after a first career, many will already have their own homes. Advice needs to be taken about whether to sell it and invest the money or to keep the house and rent it out. The size and progress of the mortgage, and your ability to keep up the payments, will be a factor.

A house of your own is security. Yes, there is an element of clergy life and the life of any Christian which should not cling to security, but there are other factors. What if the clergy person dies? It is far better for the remaining partner to have somewhere familiar to go. The price of houses continues to rise significantly, probably outstripping the returns from some types of investment. Many clergy now choose to enter the housing market before retirement in order to secure an independent choice of location for their own house.

Houses are a tie. Many clergy use up their days off travelling to maintain their house. Others say that they do not take a range of holidays because they feel obliged to go to the house they have retained or purchased. Whatever the balance in a choice of lifestyle, the security of a home and provision for retirement are concerns which clergy need to weigh up for their families, not only for themselves. Houses owned by clergy can be regarded as first homes for tax purposes and need to be registered as such. Many local authorities make a reduction in their community charges for houses not occupied for the majority of any one year.

Schooling

Few things are more stressful or more controversial than the choice of school for clergy children. Very many parishioners feel that their clergy are not really identifying with the locality if they do not send their children to the local school. Clergy agonize over this, weighing the personal and educational needs of their children against their own principles or the pressure of others. If children need special kinds of schooling, then parents need to search this out. If children have particular academic needs, then the best schools for the development of gifts and talents need to be found.

On occasions parents choose to identify with the locality above all else and children sometimes flourish there. They will certainly make more friends who are close by. Schooling can influence the jobs which clergy are prepared to take. In almost every locality, primary schools will usually be able to provide the kind of general educational grounding which children in clergy families need. It is in the area of secondary education that the differences, and needs of children, become more marked. It is now much more common for young adults, regarded as students at secondary level, to travel some distance to the right school for them.

There are sometimes particular choices which clergy, and Christian families, will want to make. The main one is the opportunity for children to attend a church school. Provision of primary education is well spread across the country and many clergy can send their children to a school of this kind. Similar secondary schools are fewer in number and very well subscribed. There is certainly something, often indefinable, about the 'ethos' of a church school which many parents want.

The other choice is to opt for private education. Some clergy will want to do this because it is their own educational background. Others will do it because they feel that the sociological area in which they choose to work should not diminish their children's chances for education. Other clergy get help from their parents or from charities and trusts to enable their children to have a private education. Some public schools give preference or bursaries to the children of clergy as a part of their foundation or trust deed.

Out-of-parish activities

Clergy do not work office hours, they rarely have job descriptions and they are not immediately accountable to anyone. This gives a great amount of freedom to clergy in how they use their time. In addition to the range of parish duties, many clergy have particular skills and interests. Within a parochial appointment there is often the opportunity to give time to a specialist, community or diocesan activity.

Clergy need to be able to choose how much time they give to out-of-parish activities. Sometimes this balance can be negotiated with a bishop or archdeacon, or on occasions the balance can be discussed with a work consultant. A measured amount of specialist work can enrich a parish ministry and give objectivity to the essentially local, parish-pump nature of life within a congregation or small community.

Diocesan committees

Every diocese has its own chosen range of specialist committees as well as its statutory ones. It enriches the life of any diocese if some of its clergy use their specialist expertise or interests in the wider life of the diocese. There are committee-sitting clergy in every diocese, just as there are the same types of people who seem to speak on every subject at synods.

A carefully chosen contribution, perhaps for not more than two sessions in the life of a committee, can be of mutual benefit. As well as giving an outside interest, a specialist contribution can provide opportunities for work and inservice training which cannot be gained from a parochial ministry with no outside interests.

Synodical government

All clergy have the opportunity to participate in the wider life of the Church. Chapter meetings of clergy are open to all those who are licensed; it impoverishes the information flow of a parish if clergy do not attend the meetings of their local chapter. It is unfortunate that these meetings often take place in the daytime and thus preclude the non-parochial clergy. However, chapter meetings are the time when clergy can get to know one another and should be places of mutual support.

Deanery synods are back in favour. As dioceses continue to devolve rapidly to deaneries, it is increasingly important that both clergy and lay people represent their parishioners at deanery synods and other deanery events. The development of the deanery appears to be one way in which the sparsity of stipendiary clergy can be accommodated. It is in the deanery that pastoral strategies are agreed and finances settled. Parish clusters, with the range of support they need, arise from deanery agreements, as do many locally based specialist appointments. Clergy need to choose to be there and make their views known, because locally originated policies will have an inevitable effect on their parishes and on the opportunities and limitations within their own work.

Diocesan synods and General Synod

Clergy are elected to diocesan synods and can use these places to contribute to national debates on social, environmental, medical and specialist topics of many kinds. Diocesan synods are the places where major budgets are set and major votes taken which influence the work of the national Church.

Some members of the diocesan synod, clergy and lay, are elected to form the Bishop's Council and Standing Committee of the Synod. It is open to all clergy to put themselves forward for these vacancies. A significant contribution can be made to diocesan life if able people are willing to separate themselves from the life of their local parish and participate in these wider spheres of government in the Church. The same is the case for those who want to offer themselves for election to the General Synod.

Hobbies and free time

Clergy are more interesting people if they have interests which take them outside church life. Hobbies are essential. The pressures and even compulsions of parish life make outside interests difficult. With the always long lists of things to do in a parish, there can emerge a sense of guilt if time is taken for oneself when needs are pressing. If time is not taken to do other things, a sense of proportion about appropriate work can be lost. God might even be revealed in yet another manifestation through a widened range of interests.

One of the choices which clergy must make is to distance themselves from their chosen life from time to time. This separation will help keep a sense of proportion. Many retired clergy discover that 'there is a big world out there'. All clergy need to discover this, even on a day off. The world does not revolve around the doings of the Church. We can forget this all too easily and our calling and ministry can be turned into an obsession by the sheer pressure placed upon us by the institution. Planned, if brief, escape should be a deliberate choice. It will help us keep a balance between those things which we need to do to be faithful to our calling and those things which intrude and prevent us from becoming the Spirit-liberated people which God intends us to be.

Part IV

What do you think of it so far?

18

Harvest time: seven characteristics of effective ministry

By a strange coincidence, the concelebrants were Angus Day and Gloria Inexelsis

How can anyone survive 40 years in the parochial ministry? Does such a span of ministry give a richness born of perspective, where experience can become a resource for an ever developing church? Or will work with four or five congregations, where development and growth may not have been the overwhelming characteristic, harden the most optimistic spirit? There are some strong themes which can be identified and named for themselves because they recur so often in the lives of clergy. Many of these characteristics are not the province of any one person or group of clergy. Few of them can be created by a minister working with a short time-span. In many ways their visible characteristics are the tips of icebergs.

They show themselves to us in ways which we can recognize but they also represent much more that is unseen.

All clergywork is done in relationship. Priesthood itself derives from the whole ministry of the people of God. A particular ministry within the Church has to be recognized by the other members of that Church or their representatives. All clergy will only be able to reflect on their ministry as they look over what has gone before. The early sense of calling to a particular Christian life, the route to training with particular colleagues, the many different parish and specialist situations in which ministers find themselves – all of these experiences create the clothing for an interior life developed through prayer, study of the scriptures and support from the sacraments. This is why I begin this final chapter with the characteristic that touches memory and leads to responses and feelings deep within the consciousness of each one of us.

1 Know your story

We each need to know and understand our own story. The mature and reflective clergyperson will neither be trapped by their past nor fearful for their future. First and foremost there will be an understood attitude to what has gone before. This includes the bad and the good, the scars and the mountain-top experiences. Previous parishes or pieces of work will be spoken of for what they were and neither worshipped as the trophy from a golden past nor condemned as the sole cause of an unfulfilled ministry. The history of priestly ministry will be celebrated and its memories passed on to newcomers and the next generation through the natural arteries of story telling which exist but can never be created. Photographs and documents from the past will be revealed with pride as a way of assisting and celebrating memory, but one particular time, people or achievement will not be venerated!

There will be times and events in the life of any priest with an element of embarrassment and stories which cannot be told in all their fullness. Within all this there will be unanswered questions about possible misjudgements – some true, most imagined, magnified and perpetuated because the reality was not talked through fully with the right people. There are right times to draw a line under such things, to say the past is the past and we shall never know the whole story. Many of those who could have given the answers will be dead and have left no written record. Others may still hold 'the secrets' and use that knowledge as their own private piece of power. There is nothing we can do about it. Exorcising ghosts is a necessity. An occurrence from the past either needs to be known about in order for even a retired clergy person to move on, or it needs to be acknowledged as no longer *directly* relevant and consigned to the past. Sometimes this needs to be done publicly, symbolically or liturgically, depending on the form of the story. There are still occasions when private confession and absolution are necessary.

In one of my own parishes I remember a lady in her eighties being deeply moved when a visiting mission group invited us all to write particular confessions, personal to ourselves, on a piece of paper. We each put our papers into an upturned dustbin lid and they were burned. The symbolism of that particular event moved to tears someone who had seen it all before but who thought she was going to have to carry some pieces of guilt to the grave.

To use your story as a resource is to be available. It is not to keep on repeating the accounts of events long gone, some of which seem to belong to another age. To be a resource is to be a person who has reflected on the experiences of ministry and identified learning experiences within them. It is the method of learning and the ability to compare then with now which can transform nostalgia and reminiscence into a treasure chest.

2 Choose to live

Even a retired clergyperson has to *want* to survive, grow and change. If the will to grow and develop is not there, then decline and ultimate stagnation are an inevitable consequence. On the one hand we know that we have a future fulfilled by the presence of the Risen Christ. On the other we struggle to work with God to reveal or establish the signs of the kingdom here on earth. Such core beliefs have to be revisited many times during a life of Christian ministry. The experienced clergyperson will have asked themselves these questions about new life, renewal, growth and change many times as their own lives have been challenged by endings or disruption. Choosing to live means choosing to move towards a future whose shape we shall recognize because we have been given its characteristics in the life, death and resurrection of Jesus Christ.

There are many veins of spirituality which can help Christian people to grow and develop, some of which feed the ministry of an ordained person. Clergy do live very much in the public eye. They cannot always show their vulnerability or even their uncertainty. Choosing to live is not choosing to learn how to put on an optimistic face in all circumstances. For me it has within it a spirituality which has explored what Mother Julian of Norwich understood and experienced when she said that 'All shall be well.' There is another much loved prayer by St Briggita of Sweden which helps us to mould a spirituality with integrity: 'Lord, show me your way and make me willing to follow it.' So, whether we are exploring as we have done in our journey through this book, working with a congregation facing conflict, or looking at models of ministry, we know that we shall never be content with what we have because God is always calling us on towards a yet unrealized and undiscovered future. We come to understand that no view of ministry will completely satisfy us but that no conflict need, ultimately, be destructive. These things cannot be if we have chosen to live as if it were possible for us to have a future which is bigger and richer in our communal life than could ever have been predicted.

3 Live with difference

It is the sign of any mature society that it can tolerate difference. We know this in reverse from the appalling atrocities which have taken place within the memory of this generation in many parts of the world. If the Christian congregation is to be a model of how community life might be, then it has to have as one of its basic characteristics the toleration of difference. There is a particular leadership place for clergy in all this. They are a model for many in the community inside and outside the Church. Clergy have privileged opportunities to say an appropriate word or to make a symbolic gesture. They can show that it is possible to live with difference and that tolerance can lead to an ability for those who differ to listen to one another. There have always been different groups within the churches. We have a terrible history of division and persecution. It may be that in this generation we can be a model of a new kind of community, where those who have real difference can live, work, play and re-create together.

Living with difference will mean that clergy working with congregations of any size know that there will be those who have very different views of what the Church is. Some will have their roots in another denomination, others will want to recreate an impossible dream of the Church from their past. Those in large congregations who hanker for the characteristics of the small, pastoral church will want to know their minister personally and expect to have a particular and regular contact. Others will expect a significant preaching ministry, while others again will want an efficiently run organization. Groups within an open congregation will have found ways of engaging in dialogue with each other about these expectations. There will be those who always feel that they are in the wrong place. Dialogue will show that only a few of us are! The 'mature' congregation led by clergy who are able to balance tolerance will have found that, in a wonderful northern European saying, 'God has put in your knapsack all you need for the journey'.

Clergy who survive in and help to grow many-faceted churches are people who have learned to balance competing expectations and live with the tension of differing opinions. 'I'm damned if I do – and I'm damned if I don't': we have all felt this at some time or other. They accept that they can never fully meet their own expectations of ministry, let alone those of widely differing groups of people within their congregations or the wider community. The minister who can live with difference is a person who will never be complacent and who will learn when to face and when to avoid conflict. They are people who have an inner ease with themselves because they have a security in their sense of God's call to a particular place and work. Such security enables them to go on and explore with a positive restlessness the questioning and dialogue necessary for difference to develop into creative community life.

4 Be a well and a spring for change

Age brings a wealth of experience and wisdom. Experience helps the wise priest to look back and bring the knowledge born from pain and struggle to those who want to put their new ideas into effect. Clergy gain particular experience about the management of change within that unique unit – the congregation. Most never know that they have this precious jewel. All our work is with people and communities who are experiencing renewal or where there is decline and a sense that direction has been lost.

Such a willingness to listen to outsiders and to search for a renewed sense of direction means that clergy will help congregations to take the management of change into their systems. The revision of aims and the establishment of targets will be common coinage. A mission statement will be the place where the vision of different groups within a congregation is focused. Clergy will lead in their willingness to review progress and show this in the way in which they order their own lives. There will certainly be times when the whole congregation and its activity groups take stock and evaluate where they are. The increasing use of work consultants and the schemes of review which dioceses and denominations establish will be welcomed. Clergy who use such assistance themselves know what resources they can draw from their own well and how to encourage, lead and feed others.

The careful, sensitive management of change involves planning. It means that a clergy and congregations develop a vision of where they want to go and devise ways of getting there through a series of manageable and achievable tasks.

Clergy who have taken the management of change into their spirituality and their working style will also be sensitive to people who want to go at a different pace. Enthusiasts will be impatient and want to forge ahead. The more cautious will enjoy the security of familiarity and advise against taking risks. Managing change within a congregation should be an exercise in attempting to take as many people as possible along with a shared vision for the future. To do this involves consultation and dialogue, and the willingness to give and take. Open debate and negotiation involve those who differ being willing both to listen and to be open to the possibility that they do not have all of the truth even on their own subject. When managed well, change has a 'win-win' feel to it, in that everyone will gain, achieve something of their own position, feel enriched by the gifts and graciousness of others, and learn more from God about themselves. Change in a theological tradition will not be all newness. It will have drawn from the spiritual and doctrinal sources of the past and used them to address a new situation. Church of England clergy, in their ordination service and at their induction to each new parish, are called upon by the Bishop 'To proclaim the faith afresh in each generation'.

Experienced clergy know that managing change takes time. Dialogue and the attempt to involve as many people as possible in a collaborative exercise are the 'long way round'. I believe that these methods of working are of the essence of the Christian gospel. The basic characteristic of any Christian community is that it values each of its members for who they are and takes each opinion and each need seriously. Such a corporate life only gains momentum when a sense of purpose is shared and sensitively managed leadership allows change and growth to have both a human and a God-shaped face.

5 Want a renewed spirituality

No effective clergyperson has a spirituality which is either wholly locked up in the past or totally turned-in on itself. Defensiveness leads to rigidity and an unwillingness to learn from those with whom we think we differ. The history of religions can be read as a history of rivalry and faction, where not only denominations but also world faiths appear to conspire to set communities and nations against one another. The other face of those same religious beliefs is not a universalism which reduces faith to a 'believe anything if it suits you' kind of religiosity. Rather, it reveals great treasures in the search for faith and meaning by people of different cultures and greatly contrasting pasts.

We live in an age when very many people are willing to explore other areas than the material elements in their lives. The clergyperson who is secure in the spirituality of their tradition, but who is willing to risk development by bringing prayer and worship into play with the religious experience of others, will convey the sense of someone who is on a lifelong spiritual journey. They will be able, in themselves, to celebrate a working life in which the spiritual dimensions of a rich ministerial life have been explored. For the many different types of clergy, this spiritual journey is a place where the searcher and the explorer meet the traditionalist and the mystic, a place where each feels themselves to be somewhere between the Mount of Transfiguration and the second distance-marker on the Emmaus Road . . .

6 Never stop learning

Life is demonstrated by the capacity to grow and change. The person committed to lifelong learning displays certain characteristics:

- continual striving to clarify and deepen the personal understanding of their lives as change takes place;
- a sense of lifelong review and discovery;
- retreats and courses as features in the never-ending process of self-understanding;
- a continuous striving to improve understandings of the vast range of possibilities contained within a call to ministry.

The learning and reflecting task within service is a mark of priests and ministers of all kinds concerned about the standard of what they can offer to God.

Learning ministers are never satisfied with their concepts or 'models'. Clergy who are alive with a hunger for learning will engage in a constant process of redefining who we are and what we are here for. Questions will continue to be asked about whether the agenda of the world is shaping the agenda for the Church and whether the behaviour of churches and congregations can influence how local and national communities understand themselves.

It is my hope that clergy committed to lifelong learning will have an energetic desire to build a shared vision with colleagues and groups wherever they find themselves. The enthusiasm of the early stages of a call to ministry will continue to break out as new ideas are shared and new experiences evaluated. Differences will not become disunion but different routes and journeys towards the common goal which the Christian community defines for itself. In this constant process of working out and dialogue, statements of core values may emerge, as will discussion of the key Christian values we share and build on as we apply principles to the pragmatism of everyday life.

Team learning is a cumulative bonus for the clergyperson committed to development who wants to maintain an inclusive and integrated congregation. The interaction of believers produces an intelligence for the group or team which exceeds that of any of the individuals within it. The joint wisdom stemming from memory and open dialogue may well be a key which opens the door for searching individuals who are willing to suspend their own assumptions in order to think together.

Much has been said about building a shared vision around all the willing members of the congregation. But a vision without the systems to put it in place is no more than a lovely picture. The learning minister for the learning congregation will be concerned about who and how, so that pathways are built to enable the workers on the journey to walk together to accomplish a particular task.

7 Celebrate your achievements

Many of the most striking pictures in the life of Jesus are those in which he eats a celebratory meal – at a wedding, with the tax-gatherers, in the Upper Room. All those involved are surprised by the difference his presence brings. The picture of the Kingdom of Heaven which he often gives us is that of a great banquet. Clergy who have worked with many congregations and groups which have shared much together and lived through agonies may well say, 'It was terrible in those meetings, but looking back I can now laugh at how serious we were.' Achievements must be celebrated and religion and worship need to have a real element of joy in them. If belief can give perspective to the troubles of family life or the world, we also need to develop ways of giving our own life within the religious community a distance and perspective, a way to celebrate what we have done and value what we have achieved.

Modesty and humility sometimes hold us back from celebrating because we think of it as boasting, or even as the result of our own efforts. Celebrations are a way of saying 'thank-you' to hard-working helpers, for prayers answered and a ministry fulfilled. Work or worship which is too inhibited is as dangerous as worship which is ecstatic in its uncontrolled exuberance.

Sometimes we just need to thank God. Just as we give thanks for all the resources and wisdom now available to help us in our attempts to learn, to grow and to be refreshed, so we need to acknowledge the source of renewal. It is only possible for us to show true appreciation if we do it in community, in communion with others. It is only with the understanding and support of those who have journeyed with us that we can be saved from our worst selves and encouraged to become the priestly people in community, the resurrection body of Christ, to which God calls us.

Bibliography and Resources

Bibliography

Adair, John, *How to Find your Vocation*. Norwich: Canterbury Press, 2000.

Adie, Michael, *Held Together, an Exploration of Coherence*. DLT: London, 1997.

Arbuckle, Gerald A., *Refounding the Church: dissent for leadership*. London: Geoffrey Chapman, 1993.

Avis, Paul, *Authority, Leadership and Conflict in the Church*. London: Mowbray, 1992.

Ball, Peter and Grundy, Malcolm, *Faith on the Way: a practical guide to the Adult Catechumenate*. London: Mowbray, 2000.

Becker, Penny Edgell, *Congregations in Conflict: cultural models of religious life*. Cambridge University Press, 1999.

Berger, Peter, *The Social Reality of Religion*. London: Faber & Faber, 1969; Penguin University Books, 1973.

Board for Mission, *Church of England: a time for sharing*. London: Church House Publishing, 1995.

Bridge, Lord, *Synodical Government in the Church of England*. London: Church House Publishing, 1997.

Brunner, Emil, *Our Faith*. London: SCM, 1936 (reprints to 1962).

Carr, Wesley, *The Priestlike Task: a model for training and developing the Church's ministry*. London: SPCK, 1985.

Clark, David (ed.), *Changing World, Unchanging Church? An agenda for Christians in public life*. London: Mowbray, 1997.

Clements, Keith, *Lovers of Discord: twentieth century theological controversies in England*. London: SPCK, 1988.

Cocksworth, Christopher and Brown, Rosalind, *Being a Priest Today: exploring priestly identity*. Norwich: Canterbury Press, 2002.

Cormack, David, *Team Spirit: people working with people.* London: MARC/Kingsway Publications, 1987.

Craig, Yvonne, *Learning for Life: a handbook of Adult Religious Education.* London: Mowbray, 1994.

Croft, Peter (ed.), *The Collaborative Church.* Barnsley: One for Christian Renewal, 1979.

Croft, Peter, *A Primer for Teams.* Loughborough: One for Christian Renewal, 1979.

Davie, Grace, *Religion in modern Europe: a memory mutates.* Oxford University Press, 2000.

Croft, Steven, *Ministry in three dimensions.* London: DLT, 1999.

Croft, Steven, *Transforming Communities: re-imagining the Church for the 21st Century.* London: DLT, 2002.

Downs, Thomas, *The Parish as a Learning Community: modeling for parish and adult growth.* New York/Toronto: Paulist Press, 1979.

Drucker, Peter, *The Age of Discontinuity: guidelines to our changing society.* London: Pan Books, 1968.

Dulles, Avery, *Models of the Church: a critical assessment of the Church in all its aspects.* Dublin: Gill & Macmillan, revised edition 1987.

Eastell, Kevin, *Appointed for Growth: a handbook of ministry development and appraisal.* London: Mowbray, 1994.

Ecclestone, Giles (ed.), *The Parish Church? Explorations in the relationship of the Church and the World.* London: Mowbray/The Grubb Institute, 1988.

General Synod of the Church of England, *Breaking New Ground: church planting in the Church of England.* London: Church House Publishing, 1994.

Edmondson, Christopher, *Fit to Lead: sustaining effective ministry in a changing world.* London: DLT, 2002.

Francis, James M. M. and Francis, Leslie (eds), *Tentmaking: perspectives on self-supporting ministry.* Leominster: Gracewing, 1998.

Francis, Leslie and Jones, Susan H. (eds), *Psychological Perspectives on Christian Ministry.* Leominster: Gracewing, 1996.

Freire, Paulo, *Pedagogy of the Oppressed.* London: Sheed & Ward, 1972; Penguin Books, 1972.

General Synod of the Church of England, *For Such a Time as This: a renewed diaconate in the Church of England.* London: Church House Publishing, 2001.

Edmondson, Christopher, *Minister – Love Thyself.* Cambridge: Grove Books, 2000.

Gorringe, Tim, *Alan Ecclestone: Priest as Revolutionary.* Sheffield: Cairns Publications, 1994.

Green, Laurie, *Let's Do Theology: a pastoral cycle resource book.* London: Mowbray, 1990.

Greenwood, Robin, *Transforming Priesthood: a new theology of mission and ministry.* London: SPCK, 1994.

Greenwood, Robin, *Practising Community: the task of the local church.* London: SPCK, 1996.

Greenwood, Robin, *Transforming Church: liberating structures for ministry.* London: SPCK, 2002.

Grundy, Malcolm, *Understanding Congregations.* London: Mowbray, 1998.

Habgood, John, *Faith and Uncertainty.* London: DLT, 1997.

Handy, Charles, *Understanding Organisations.* London: Penguin Books, fourth edition 1993.

Handy, Charles, *The Empty Raincoat: making sense of the future.* London: Hutchinson, 1994.

Handy, Charles, *Gods of Management.* London: Arrow, 1995.

Harvey-Jones, John, *Making it Happen: reflections on leadership.* London: Collins, 1988.

Hastings, Adrian, *The Shaping of Prophecy, Passion, Perception and Practicality.* London: Geoffrey Chapman, 1995.

Higginson, Richard, *Transforming Leadership: a Christian approach to management.* London: SPCK, 1996.

Kuhrt, Gordon (ed.), *Ministry Issues for the Church of England.* London: Church House Publishing, 2001.

Lovell, George, *The Church and Community Development.* London: Grail/Chester House Publications for Avec, 1972; revised editions 1980 and 1992.

Lovell, George, *Analysis and Design.* London: Burns & Oates, 1994.

Lovell, George and Widdicombe, Catherine, *Churches and Communities: an approach to development in the local church.* London: Search Press, 1978 and 1986.

Martineau, Jeremy, *The Vicar is Leaving.* Stoneleigh: Arthur Rank Centre, 1998.

Morisy, Ann, *Beyond the Good Samaritan: community ministry and mission.* London: Mowbray, 1997.

Nazir-Ali, Michael, *Shapes of the Church to Come*. London: Kingsway Publications, 2001.

Nelson, John (ed.), *Management and Ministry: appreciating contemporary issues*. London: Canterbury Press for MODEM, 1996.

Nelson, John (ed.), *Managing and Leading: challenging questions for the churches*. London: Canterbury Press for MODEM, 1988.

Pattinson, Stephen, *The Faith of the Managers: when management becomes religion*. London: Cassell, 1997.

Peters, Thomas J. and Waterman, Robert H., *In Search of Excellence: lessons from America's best-run companies*. New York: Harper & Row, 1982.

Peters, Thomas J., *Liberation Management: necessary disorganization for the nanosecond nineties*. New York: Alfred A. Knopf, 1992.

Platten, Stephen, James, Graham and Chandler, Andrew (eds), *New Soundings: essays on developing tradition*. London: DLT, 1997.

Reed, Bruce, *The Dynamics of Religion: process and movement in Christian churches*. London: DLT, 1978.

Reeves, Donald, *Down to Earth: a new vision for the church*. Mowbray, 1997.

Rudge, Peter, *Order and Disorder in Organisations*. Australia: for CORAT, 1990.

Russell, Anthony, *The Clerical Profession*. London: SPCK, 1980.

Russell, Anthony, *The Country Parson*. London: SPCK, 1993.

Schillebeeckx, Edward, *Ministry: a case for change*. London: SCM, 1981.

Turnbull, Michael (Chair), *Working as One Body: the report of the Archbishop's commission on the organisation of the Church of England*. London: Church House Publishing, 1995.

Wagner, C. Peter, *Leading your Church to Growth*. London: MARC Europe, 1984.

Warren, Robert, *Building Missionary Congregations*. London: Church House Publishing, 1995.

Resources

Chapter 1: Who would be a priest?

Cocksworth, Christopher and Brown, Rosalind, *Being a Priest Today*. Canterbury Press, 2002.

Duffy, Eamon, *The Voices of Morebath*. Yale University Press, 2001.

Forder, Charles, *The Parish Priest Today*. Out of print.

Francis, James M.M. and Francis, Leslie, *Tentmaking: perspectives on self-supporting ministry*. Gracewing, 1998.

Herbert, George, *A Priest to the Temple or the Country Parson*. In John N. Wall (ed.), *George Herbert: The Country Parson, The Temple*; Classics of Western Spirituality, SPCK, 1981.

Greenwood, Robin, *Transforming Priesthood*. SPCK, 1994.

Greenwood, Robin, *Transforming Church: liberating structures for ministry*. SPCK, 2002.

Grundy, Malcolm, *Understanding Congregations*. Mowbray, 1998.

Khurt, Gordon (ed.), *Ministry Issues: mapping the trends for the Church of England*. Church House Publishing, 2001.

Küng, Hans, *Why Priests?* Collins, 1972.

Ramsey, Michael, *The Christian Priest Today*. SPCK, seventh impression 1999.

Schillebeeckx, Edward, *Ministry*. SCM, 1980.

Chapter 8: Glittering prizes

Relevant books and reports (all reports are available from Church House Publishing, Church House, Great Smith Street, London SW1P 3NZ):

Code of Practice for Senior Church Appointments. GS 1019, 1992.

Working with the Spirit: choosing diocesan bishops. GS 1405, 2001.

Resourcing Bishops: the first report of the Archbishops' Review Group on bishops' needs and resources. 2001.

Working as one Body: report of the Archbishops' Commission of the organisation of the Church of England. 1995.

Heritage and Renewal: report of the Archbishops' Commission of Cathedrals. 1994.

Synodical Government in the Church of England: a review. GS
    1252, 1997.
A Handbook for New Archdeacons. Originally compiled by Hugh
    Buckingham and revised; available from Revd Dr John Mantle,
    Cowley House, 9 Little College Street, London S W 1 P 3 S H.

Chapter 10: Parishes great and small

Oswald, Roy M., 'How to minister effectively in family, pastoral,
    programme and corporate sized churches'. Action Information,
    Alban Institute, March/April 1991.

Chapter 11: The archdeacon says

Books which can act as important sources of reference:
The Charities Act 1993 and the PCC. Church House Publishing,
    2nd edition 2001.
Data Protection: Notification Handbook. Data Protection Notifi-
    cation Department, 2001.
*Policy in Child Protection: a policy document by the House of
    Bishops.* Church House Publishing, 1999.
*Meeting the Challenge: how the church should respond to sex
    offenders.* Church House Publishing, 1999.
*Care of Churches and Ecclesiastical Jurisdiction Measure: Code of
    Practice.* Church House Publishing, 1993.
Department of the Environment, *The Care of Redundant Churches.*
    HMSO, 1990.
The Churchyards Handbook. Church House Publishing, many
    editions to 2002.
*Through the Roof: straightforward advice on how to make your
    church welcoming to disabled people.* Through the Roof,
    Global House, Ashley Avenue, Epsom, Surrey K T 1 8 5 A D.
    www.throughtheroof.org
Joint Grant Scheme for Churches and other Places of Worship.
    Heritage Lottery Fund, 7 Holbein Place, London S W 1 W 8 N R.
    and English Heritage, 23 Savile Row, London W 1 X 1 A B.
Church Health and Safety Policy. Ecclesiastical Insurance Group,
    Beaufort House, Brunswick Road, Gloucester G L 1 1 J Z.

Chapter 12: Managing the vicarage tea party

Training and resource organizations:

MODEM: contact the Membership Secretary, Mr Peter Bates, Carselands, Woodmancote, Henfield, West Sussex BN5 9SS; peter@bateshouse.freeserve.co.uk; www.modem.uk.com

The Leadership Institute: The Secretary, 15 Stockwell Street, Cambridge CB1 3ND; jenny.joice@ntlworld.com; www.tli.org.uk

The Edward King Institute for Ministry Development, PO Box 4, Longhope SPDO, Gloucestershire GL17 QYP.

The Grubb Institute, Miss Jean Hutton, The Grubb Institute, Cloudesley Street, London N1 OHU; info@grubb.org.uk

Chapter 13: All together now

Working as One Body. Report of the Church of England Synod; Church House Publishing, 1995.

The Sign We Give. Report from the Working Party on Collaborative Ministry, Catholic Bishop's Conference of England and Wales; Matthew James Publishing, 1995.

Chapter 15: Power, conflict and service

Gillian Stamp, *The Enhancement of Ministry in Uncertainty.* Brunel Institute of Organization and Social Studies, Published Paper, 1993.

Chapter 16: Spirituality and a Rule of Life

Robert K. Greenleaf, *Servant Ministry.* Gracewing/Paulist Press, 1991.

Robert Innes, *Personality Indicators and the Spiritual Life.* Grove Spirituality Series 57, 1996.

Kenneth Leech, *Soul Friend: a study of spirituality.* Sheldon, 1977.

Harold Miller, *Finding a Personal Rule of Life.* Grove Spirituality Series 8, 1987.

Index

Printed in the United Kingdom
by Lightning Source UK Ltd.
111756UKS00001B/64-123